In the Name of God, the
Merciful and Compassionate

Walking with God

How to Achieve Health, Happiness, and Fulfillment through Spiritual Healing

James Keeley

Rosewood Press
99 Rosewood Lane
Berkeley Springs, WV 25411

Text and cover design: Jonathan Gullery
RJ Communications

ISBN 10: 0-9779424-0-6
ISBN 13: 978-0-9779424-0-4

Library of Congress Control Number: 2006902993

Printed in the United States of America

Table of Contents

Acknowledgements

This book is a product of every caring hand that has helped my on my journey. I would especially like to thank all of the students and faculty at the University of Spiritual Healing and Sufism, their experience and insight can be seen all over this book. I owe a debt of gratitude to my guide and teacher, Sidi al Jamal, who showed me the way home and to my family for all of their love and support throughout this process. May God bless them all and grant them peace.

Introduction

In writing this book, it is my intention to give thanks to the Most High for all that I have received over the past ten years of walking in this way. I also wish to share teachings and insights that have allowed both me and the people I have had the privilege to help discover a world of immeasurable beauty and richness in the face of our most difficult challenges.

Time and time again, a constant refrain I have heard over the last several years from the people in our workshops is, "Where are these teachings written down?" This is my attempt at putting down in plain, practical language the spiritual teachings I have gleaned from my journey. Although it is based in the teachings of the Sufi path, a mystical tradition going back thousands of years, it contains insights that I have found helpful from the hospital bed to the living room and the boardroom. This book is a distillation from many sources and teachers into a hopefully simple and accessible format that will allow you to discover a path of harmony using your challenges as the catalyst for that discovery. It is a message to every heart that speaks of the nearness and availability of Divine love, guidance, and support. This message reaches beyond religious barriers to the spiritual transformation that all of us go through on our journey to wholeness.

It is my prayer that I have used words and ideas that will

touch your heart and allow you to realize the sweetness of walking with God. Any help, guidance, or insight you may find in this book is a gift from the Divine. Any mistakes or omissions only come from myself.

As you read, take some time to go over the chapter summaries and try the exercises. The first six chapters will give you the necessary understandings to apply the process of spiritual healing to any challenge in your life. Chapter seven puts the whole process together and lays out the steps in an easy to follow format. The last four chapters explain how to live a life of balance and will guide you through the process of supporting others.

When I set out to write this book, I thought I would be expanding the message of spiritual healing into new circles. One day in prayer, however, I received an image in my heart that clearly showed me that this book was a net that God was building for the people He was calling home. So much for new circles. Well, people of the net, this book is for you.

The human being is a guest house,
Every morning a new arrival.
A joy, a depression, some difficulty,
Some momentary awareness comes as an unexpected visitor
Welcome and entertain them all!
Even if they are a crowd of sorrows who violently sweep your house
empty of your furniture, still, treat each guest honorably.
He may be clearing you out for some new delight.
Be grateful for whoever comes, because each has been sent
As a guide from beyond.
Rumi

Chapter One

The Foundation of Spiritual Healing

Man is a product of his thoughts,
what he believes, he becomes
—Mahatma Gandhi.

Over the past ten years I have had the chance to train healers and work directly with people in individual and group settings. Because spiritual healing is not most people's first stop (that is, they have tried several other modalities before showing up at a spiritual healer's office), I've been able to observe a fundamental difference between the people who heal and those who stay stuck in chronic patterns.

Working with many people (for example, those suffering from physical disease, emotional and mental conditions, relationship issues, or work-related struggles) gave me insight into the overall process that each goes through. I've discovered that people get sick on a variety of levels because we are more than just our physical bodies. We are a combination of the sensations we experience, the thoughts we think, the emotions we feel, the relationships we are in, the jobs we do, and the environment we live in. None of these areas of our lives exists in isolation, and I have found that, if one of these areas is suffering, the rest are also affected.

The most striking difference I have discovered between those who have healed and those who continued to suffer is that those who healed had or developed a relationship to Spirit. By this, I mean they had an inner connection to something larger than themselves. For some people, this relationship is with God. For others, it is with the universe or love. Regardless of what they called it however, each of these people had faith.

What they had faith in was a benevolent or Divine presence that cared for them in their times of pain, offered insight, and supported them in coming into balance with what was happening in their lives. These people discovered their problems and challenges were not random or arbitrary and they were not alone in facing them. Despite these obstacles, they were able to discover a resource that carried them through difficult times. This resource enabled them to face their challenges as experiences they had to go through in order to grow as individuals, not as problems they had to eliminate. They realized there was meaning behind what was happening to them and reached out to the support and guidance of the Divine to discover it. Their faith allowed them to be fully present and acknowledge their painful experiences until they were given what they needed to leave their pain behind.

It is not that the people who had faith didn't get upset; they just didn't allow upset feelings to guide their actions. They were willing to face what was upsetting them and all these experiences represented while reaching out to a beneficent force for guidance and care. They felt part of a grand plan, were able to sense or receive guidance and were willing to let go of how they thought their lives should look and play their part.

Most importantly, when the events of life hurt them, the people who had faith turned to the Divine for support, insight, and guidance rather than just looking for a way out. Time and time again, I found truth in the old teaching that tells us "the way out is through".

The Foundation of Healing

So many modalities of healing are available to us today. Everything from allopathic medical care to homeopathy, body-work, psychotherapy, nutrition, and many others are employed to change states of disease and unhappiness to ones of health and balance. If a person is sick, these modalities seek to find out what is causing his or her sickness and what remedy will return him or her to health. While great attention is placed on remedying the symptoms and reasons for peoples' suffering, their experience or what it means for them to be going through these times of pain is often overlooked. Not only does someone going through a serious illness or difficult life event have to contend with what is happening, he or she also has to deal with what it feels like to be going through these events and the painful beliefs and conclusions these experiences generate.

There is a difference between the events of our lives and what upsets us about those events. Inside of every upsetting situation is what it means to the person going through it. Each of us is unique in our relationship to life. What upsets one person about being sick or having a hard time in a relationship may not pose problems or be difficult for another. Two people in the same situation can be upset about what is happening for completely different reasons. Regardless of what we are upset about, all of us have one thing in common. We are upset because we feel as a given situation cuts us off from what we need and consciously or unconsciously believe this forces us to live in an unfulfilling way. For example, a person diagnosed with a serious illness may be upset about losing his mobility because he feels helpless. To this person, feeling helpless means that he is a useless burden on others. Someone going through a hard time in relationship may be upset because she feels let down and decides this means she cannot rely on anyone.

Spiritual healing takes the radical stance of saying that our experience and what we believe an illness or challenging situation means for us is just as important as what is happening and the causes of these struggles. Acknowledging and resolving the painful experiences that are associated with our challenges is the key to healing because what we decide a situation means for us sets the tone for all of our thoughts and actions.

This brings us to two pyramids that illustrate the healing process. The first shows how we receive and interpret the events of our lives. At the top are our difficult situations or challenges. Underneath these situations is what upsets us about what is happening, that is, our problems. Finally, at the base of the pyramid are our issues, which indicate our experiences and what we believe these problems mean for us. At the foundation of this pyramid, we find the real reasons we are upset about what is happening.

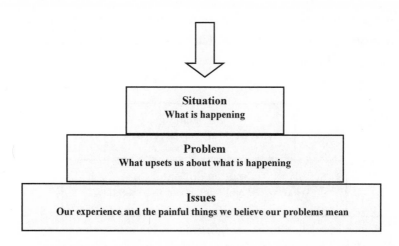

When we believe an upsetting situation means something negative for us, it feels as if we must live without what we need. Whether or not we feel as if we have what we need in a given situation provides the foundation for all of our emotions, thoughts, and actions. It is easy to feel calm, hopeful, trusting, peaceful, and certain that things are going to be all right when we experience ourselves as being cared for and having what we need. These positive feelings are passed on into our lives in the form of positive words and actions. When we feel unsupported, it is very easy to feel distress, anger, sadness, fear, hopelessness, and misery. These negative feelings are passed on into our lives as well. Is it any wonder that, when we are upset about what is happening, believing we are cut off from what we need, thinking upset thoughts, and responding to our lives with actions based in pain, that we often get more to be upset about?

The second pyramid has to do with how we respond to the events of our lives. In this pyramid, we see how our experience of a situation sets the tone for our feelings and beliefs, which impacts how we respond to events. This pyramid starts at the bottom on the spiritual level. Each part is supported and influenced by the one beneath.

Physical
What we do and say in response

Emotional/Mental
What we feel and think about that situation

Spiritual
Whether or not we feel as if we have what we need in a situation

For ages, healing traditions have been telling us that what we feel, think, say, and do affects our well-being. Because what we believe about the circumstances of our lives creates either a positive or negative experience that gets passed on to our feelings, thoughts, and actions, disharmony from lower in the pyramid can affect everything from our health and livelihood to our relationships and social interactions.

I was working with a client who was diagnosed with uterine cancer. What upset her about having cancer was that she did not feel ready to die, but she felt she did not have a choice. Because she did not have a choice, she believed there was nothing to do except prepare for the end. This belief set the tone for depressing thoughts and feelings. She began withdrawing from life. When she discovered her belief that she had to prepare for the end, she realized it was taking the living out of life for her. Upon reflection, she realized that preparing for the end never felt right in her heart. Instead, she felt guided to embrace and enjoy every moment. To this day, she continues to outlive her prognosis.

The foundational principle of spiritual healing is that, while difficult things do happen to us, none of these things cuts us off from the support of the Divine. Behind every situation we go through is the hand of the Divine giving us what we need to move through in harmony. There are many times in life, however, when we are not aware of this support. Getting sick, having trouble in our relationships, losing a loved one, and enduring other painful events can be devastating and leave us feeling cut off and alone. What we do in these moments determines whether or not the foundation of our pyramid is one of harmony and balance or of discord and instability

Spiritual healing focuses on the foundations of both pyramids by connecting us to the love and support of the Divine in painful situations. When this support touches these places of pain, our experiences are guided into those of balance. Healing then happens. This healing is passed on to our emotions and thoughts in the form of peace. This peace is displayed in our bodies and lives as health and balance.

Remembrance

The practice of reaching out to Divine support and guidance is called remembrance. It is called remembrance because we are reminding ourselves of the availability of Divine support in a situation that has caused us to forget it.

People refer to the Divine by many different names. For some, it is God. For others, it is Yahweh. Other people refer to the Divine as Great Spirit or Universal Love. For some, the name is Allah. Whatever name we use, it is important for the practice of the remembrance that it represents the highest, most beautiful reality we can conceive of. If we are lost in the desert, why not ask directions from the one who created every grain of sand and cactus? It is important for our remembrance that we not use a name that represents a single quality of the Divine, such as strength or compassion. Instead, we should use a name that encompasses all of the qualities. Our name for the Divine should remind us that the limitless love, support, and guidance of the Divine are available to us, even in our most trying times.

Albert Einstein said the most important question one must answer is whether or not the universe is friendly. We can just as easily substitute "God" for "universe," but feeling like we are at odds with the universe and cut off from what we need creates sickness at the foundation of our beings. I have seen that, when this foundation is healthy, everything else follows in health. When it is sick, the rest of our lives soon follow.

I was once sharing this quote from Albert Einstein with a class. One of the students said the most interesting part of the question of whether or not the universe is friendly is that, however you answer it, you are correct. His statement took me back a bit a first until I realized what he was saying was incredibly profound. How we answer this question makes it so in only one place, our experience. Because that is the only place we will ever live, how we shape it affects everything else in our lives

Spiritual healing is more than positive thinking or looking on the bright side of things. It is genuinely experiencing the love, guidance, and support of God in a situation that previously felt terrible because of what we believed it meant for us. In fact, as soon as this support is felt, the label of "difficult" often falls away. We then begin to move forward in balance.

We can spend so much time avoiding what hurts, we never discover this inner resource of Divine support and instead continue to look outside for answers. It is easy to overlook our experiences and not realize that, at the foundation of our beings, we believe we are cut off from what we need and must respond in an unfulfilling way. Our focus is often on changing the circumstances that are upsetting us, but spiritual healing shows us that we must first come into harmony with what is happening and act from a sense of balance before our actions will lead to real, lasting healing. Often, people go from one treatment to another to try to get whatever is hurting in their lives to stop instead of facing their pain and, in that aching, reach out to the Divine for support.

Working only on the physical or mental/emotional levels represents a gap in the way many people approach healing. We often want to try to change what is happening with our bodies or how we are living our lives or acting in relationship without addressing the experience of the person who is displaying these symptoms or behaviors. By first focusing on our experience in times of suffering and consciously connecting with the love and support of the Divine, the foundation for all of our actions becomes one of peace.

> *I had a client who suffered from severe anxiety. Whenever he got around groups of people, he would become incredibly distraught. To him, this meant he was unfit for public interactions and he had to hide himself away. This made him feel extremely uncomfortable and fearful of interactions when he was unable to hide, which further exacerbated his problem. To help his anxiety, he tried all types of interventions. Through the work of spiritual healing, he was able to see that believing he was unfit for public interaction was at the root of his anxiety. As he acknowledged this and reached out to the Divine, he discovered that what he had been telling himself was not true. It was only a conclusion he had drawn that was based on experiences from his past. This represented a huge breakthrough for him. In several sessions, his anxiety was alleviated.*

Many times, the negative things we believe a situation means can make us more miserable than what is actually happening. We often believe these unsupportive issues for a long time without reaching out for more. Years ago, my teacher Sidi al Jamal shared with me a sublime poem that exquisitely captures our dilemma.

> *Your sickness is from you but you do not know*
> *Your cure is within you but you do not see*
> *You think you are a small star*
> *when you actually contain the whole universe.*

The sickness that is from us, comes from the negative meanings we assign to difficult events. The cure within us is our connection to the Divine that can guide us into harmony, regardless of what is happening in our lives. Our belief that our well-being is based in events is the small star that is contrasted with the truth that Spirit always suffices us. This truth allows us to embrace a whole universe of experience and live a life of balance.

Connecting to the Divine

When we forget about our connection to the Divine, we are left without the resources to move through what pains us. The self that experienced a situation negatively for us unconsciously locks us into that experience. As a result, we unknowingly create our lives and make decisions based on an assumption that we are not whole. When we live as if this is the only perspective we have to draw upon, life can become an upsetting struggle to find balance.

No one knows what the human being needs like the Creator of the human being. If we are going to realize true happiness and fulfillment, we must cultivate our relationship with our Creator. When we allow the insights from the Divine to inform our lives, we are moved by grace into harmony with whatever life brings. From this state of being, our thoughts and emotions become clear. What we need to do, change, or release in order to heal becomes apparent. Spiritual healing does not take the place of other modalities. Instead, it becomes the basis on which all other treatments rest. Rather than avoiding what is causing us pain, we discover a center of well-being in the midst of our challenges that moves our choices in the direction of wholeness. For the people with whom I have had the privilege to work, returning to and living from an experience of connection made the difference between moving forward into balance and staying stuck in chronic patterns or disease states.

> *I have seen and heard of so many instances where people looked everywhere for relief. They tried everything. When their situation finally got too bad to handle, they broke down and put their faith in God. They usually say something to the effect of, "I feel as if I am at the end of my rope. I don't know how this is going to turn out, but I am putting my faith in you to bring me through it." It always amazes me that what these people need in order to heal shows up after a prayer of this type. The right treatment, relationship, job, or situation seems to come out of nowhere. When God moves us into a state of peace, what we need on the outside soon shows up as a reflection of that peace.*

Turning Inside

Focusing on what is happening and how we got there rather than on our experience and what we believe a situation means for us is called living on the outside. Our attention is outside, involved in things and events, as opposed to being inside with an awareness of our internal response. In order to access the power of our spiritual connection, we must change our point of view from looking outside to looking inside. Now, this is no small statement. To begin to look inside, we must let go of wishing that things were different and face the fact that this is what we are being given right now. Whatever is happening is meant to happen, even if we think we are the cause of our own suffering and should know better. We must momentarily release our ideas of right and wrong as well as fair and unfair. This allows us to be in a relationship with the events of our lives.

We discover that we have what we need in every moment when we stop arguing with the flow of events, become conscious of our experience, and support that experience by turning inside to receive Divine care. When we consciously connect to Divine support, we are able to embrace the process of life through all of its ups and downs and flow with the changes because we experience a sense of peace and well-being that is available, regardless of what happens to us. One of my colleagues likes to say that all of us only have one core issue, and that is whether or not we are experiencing the love and support of the Divine at our core. When we are experiencing this support, we feel at peace, think positive thoughts, speak positive words, and take positive actions that all lead in the direction of healing. We are then able to base our well-being on the availability of God's support instead of on things and events. Experiencing this stream of love allows us to be fully alive and present for all that life brings.

The only thing that truly limits us is what
we don't yet know about Divine love.

The Journey of Healing

Both pain and joy play a part in our development as people. Can you think of anyone you truly admire who did not endure adversity? There is more to our lives than having everything go the way we would like. There is our journey as individuals.

Spiritual healing is different from other forms of healing in one fundamental aspect. While most healing has to do with trying to figure out how not to hurt, spiritual healing is based on the belief that, when we hurt, God guides and supports us into becoming individuals who have the resources to walk through that pain and leave it behind. In the healing process, we grow as people. The events of our lives put us into experiences and situations that cause us to reach past who we have been. These circumstances bring up the places inside of us where we unaware of Divine support. Difficult events often reveal the painful beliefs and decisions we have previously made in our lives that are contributing to our problems today. As we walk with God through these situations, our relationship with the Divine deepens. We also release the things that don't serve us or really matter and discover new and more fulfilling ways of living.

Modern research tells us that one of the most important factors in people recovering from life-threatening illnesses and traumatic situations is their ability to reinvent themselves. Yet, we often want to hurry up and get better or get over this argument so we can get back to the lives that made us sick or led to our unhappiness in the first place. As we face the upsetting situations of our lives and acknowledge the places inside of us that don't feel as if they have what they need, illness, relationship troubles, problems at work, and, ultimately, our lives become the catalyst for discovering the fullness of our spiritual potential.

With this understanding, we begin to realize that life is not about things and events going any one way. Rather, life is about experiencing the fullness that is available to us, regardless of what happens. When we turn from the outside to the inside, we accept that growth is a natural part of existence and the events in our lives are the catalysts for that growth. We understand that difficult things don't happen to us because something went wrong. Rather, it is because we are not finished growing. The next and more difficult idea we need to embrace is that we do not know what we are growing into and therefore do not know what experiences are needed to catalyze that transformation. When we can accept these two ideas, we can stop resisting the things that hurt and begin traveling on a path that not only leads to healing, but nurtures and enlightens our very selves.

The Key Ingredient

The true beauty of spiritual healing goes far beyond relieving symptoms or improving relationships. These are just the parts of our lives that get our attention. When we regain spiritual alignment, every area of our lives improves. Our entire existence is built upon either an experience of love and purpose that comes from feeling connected to the Divine or an experience of separation. All of our actions, thoughts, beliefs, interactions, and relationships are based on this principle. Divine love is more than just affection. It is the experience of support and guidance that leads us in a wholesome and fulfilling direction. Receiving this key ingredient at our core allows everything else to fall into place.

When we remember and listen to God, we can receive the support and guidance necessary to move through what we were unable to move through alone. The same situation we judged as terrible going into dramatically changes when we open to the Divine. I have heard so many people say that cancer or some other challenging experience turned out to be the best thing that ever happened to them. When they got through their crisis or disease process, so many things in their lives had changed for the better. Everything from how they relate to themselves and others to what they are living for and placing their focus on was transformed. Somehow, the thing that looked so wrong in the beginning turned out to be the process that catalyzed their becoming the person who could receive what their hearts were truly longing for. They could only shake their heads and praise the Divine.

The process of spiritual healing becomes the path we walk into deeper and more fulfilling experience of life. Healing is essentially discovering and aligning with the support of the Divine that is guiding us into a greater experience of fullness from behind every situation. We honor our symptoms and listen to them as messengers. We embrace our bodies as vessels of the Divine presence. We allow our thoughts and feelings to become paramount in our interest. When we realize the situations we face are the raw materials for spiritual transformation and acknowledge what they represent for us, our lives become our spiritual path.

As human beings, we have an incredible capacity to carry suffering. We can live with all types of difficult experiences until something finally gets our attention. Usually what gets our attention is pain of a kind that we cannot ignore. For some of us, that pain manifests as physical disease. For others, it is difficult relationships. For some, it is problems with work or money. Whatever it is, it hurts, and we cannot make it go away. The things that upset us in these times of hardship are often feelings we have had many times before. Only now, we cannot cope with or ignore them any longer.

It is called a healing process because it takes time. While instant, miraculous healings are known to occur, most of the lasting healing happens because of an investment in time and energy into this journey. The current state of our lives is the result of years of actions and beliefs in the form of inner and outer expression. As we replace unhealthy actions and beliefs with healthy ones based in spiritual connection, our lives heal. Healing is more than relieving symptoms. It is returning to the experience of love, unity, and purpose at our core and experiencing the fullness of our spirit. Our relationships, lives, and health improve as a natural result of that experience.

Spiritual traditions tell us that "after every hardship comes ease" and "this, too, will pass." Developing our connection to the Divine firmly establishes us in a beautiful life by bringing us into relationship with a resource that guides us into harmony, regardless of what is happening. When we are aligned with the Divine, we can move through anything. No matter what we are going through, it is important not to believe the parts of ourselves that tell us there is no hope. The love and support of the Divine reaches every heart. We do not need to fix what is broken with us or find a way out. We simply must acknowledge our need for guidance and place our painful issues in the hands of the Divine. In my years as a healer, two things have amazed me: a person's ability to carry suffering and the miraculous power of spiritual alignment to bring them through anything and wash that suffering away.

Chapter Summary

1. Difficult things happen to us in our lives.
2. None of these things cuts us off from Divine support.
3. In times of hardship, it is the painful things we believe about what is happening that need this support.
4. The process of reminding ourselves of the availability of Divine support is called remembrance.
5. When we acknowledge difficult experiences and open to Divine insight, our issues and experiences of a painful situation are guided into harmony and healing happens.
6. This healing is transferred to our emotions, thoughts, beliefs, words, and actions and leads to balance and well-being in our lives.
7. Through spiritual healing, not only do we resolve our issues, we also grow as people and release the ways of living that no longer serve us.

Exercise: A spiritual workout

The following practice is meant to be done every day to strengthen your connection to the Divine. This time is meant to water and nurture your spirit as well as deepen your pathway of connection to the Divine so it is more easily recalled in times of pain and celebrated in times of joy.

1. To begin, simply become aware of yourself. Take an inventory. Taking a moment to become aware of these various aspects of yourself, answer the following questions:
   a. How am I doing?

b. How does my body feel from head to toe?

c. Are there areas of tension?

d. How are my emotions? Is anything upsetting me?

e. How are my thoughts? Are there any thoughts that I am preoccupied with?

2. Acknowledge your sensations, thoughts, and emotions. Open them to receiving Divine support. Let your entire being know its job is simply to receive for the next period. Begin remembrance by softly repeating the name of the Divine you feel most comfortable with to yourself. You are both invoking the Divine and bringing your awareness to its constant presence.

3. Breathe and receive whatever is available to you from the Divine presence as it comes into your awareness.

4. Feel how adding the awareness of the Divine presence into your experience changes your body, emotions, and thoughts. Stay conscious of these changes, and continue repeating your name for the Divine for at least fifteen minutes.

5. After you finish, go back and notice what has changed in your body, emotions, and thoughts.

6. Take a moment to both thank the Divine for what you have received and thank yourself for taking the time for this practice.

Spiritual healing is based on receiving support and guidance from the Divine. Spending time in remembrance every day develops a sensitivity and receptiveness to this ever-present support. Over time, you will find that this presence is increasingly in your awareness until you are finally never without it.

The practice of having to remind yourself eventually becomes the experience of having remembered. Then, your faith becomes certain.

Chapter Two

Turning to the Divine

Every loving thought is true; anything else is a cry for
healing, no matter how it presents itself.

Spiritual healing is built on the understanding that, when
we take a step toward the Divine, the Divine runs toward us. It
is not always easy, however, to take that step. When something
happens that is painful for us, it goes against what we would
have chosen for ourselves. In these moments, we can be caught
up in our own feelings and opinions about the situation and
forget about the love and care of the Divine that is available to
us. What a painful situation means to us and the resulting experience can leave us feeling as if we are cut off from what we
need. As a result, we often spend our energy resisting what is
painful or striving toward what we would prefer.

In order to receive the Divine's guidance and support, we
must first become aware of our experience and what our selves
are telling us a situation means. In spiritual healing, we make
a distinction between problems and issues. A problem is what
upsets us about the things that happen in our lives. Issues point
to our experiences and beliefs about what these problems mean
for us. For instance, a person may be suffering from some
chronic illness, but he is bothered because nothing he does is

making it go away (problem). He then decides that this means he just has to bear it (issue). This conclusion creates its own little world. He feels and looks a certain way when he is bearing it. Uncomfortable elements and forces exert themselves and what he needs feels absent.

The conclusions of our issues are actually decisions. They are what we believe a situation means for us. Therefore, they determine the course of action we believe we must take because of our problems. Because our issues are what we have decided to do, they affect our entire physical, mental, and emotional health. Our bodies and minds literally take on the shape of our issues and create an environment of suffering rather than facilitating healing.

If we take our issues at face value, there are plenty of reasons to be upset about what is happening. How can we be at peace when we have decided we have to live with less than wholeness? In short, our issues feel bad. Spiritual healing indicates that, if what we believe about a situation is unsupportive, we do not have the whole truth. If the conclusions we draw about the events of our lives (issues) cause us to feel incomplete, then we are in need of Divine guidance. I often refer to this process as getting a spiritual second opinion. We admit to the pain in our version of events and open to the Divine, saying, "What I believe this situation means for me is not supportive. Therefore, I know I am in need of guidance and support. I place myself in Your Hands to receive this guidance and care."

I was discussing this process with a client. I was asking him about what he received from his connection to the Divine. He answered that the responses he was getting were really making a difference in his life. He went on to say that, while he couldn't be sure he was hearing the "Voice of God," he was getting something a heck of a lot better than what he had been telling himself.

Admitting that we feel cut off from what we need in a given situation and that what we believe about it does not feel supportive, makes room for Divine revelation. Acknowledging we are in need of guidance and support empties the cup of our awareness. If our cup is filled with our issues, there is no room for anything else. In order to truly empty our cup, we must be willing to experience how believing our issues really feels and realize how they affect us. When, through our own experience, we are certain the beliefs of our issues do not serve us but rather injure or diminish who we are, it is easier to release them and open to spirit.

Water Flows to Low-lying Places

We are deaf to the guidance of God until we acknowledge and experience what a situation is like for us. In order to receive the water of Divine support and guidance, we must be willing to be a low-lying place. This means turning to God with an awareness of our own need for support and guidance. We do this sincerely and humbly. When we are willing to acknowledge that something is upsetting us, sincerity comes naturally from the genuine discomfort with that situation. (We know we are in trouble). Humility comes from knowing we are in need of guidance. (We don't have the answers because what we are telling ourselves this situation means is not supportive).

There are two sides to accepting and facing the difficult events of our lives. We must be willing to face what is happening and accept our feelings about it. Only when both of these aspects are considered are we truly present with a situation. We will never know that we are being given what we need to get through a situation until we are consciously in it with all of our painful issues and turn to God from that experience. We cannot jump over experiencing the pain of our issues because we are in need of guidance and support. We are not just feeding ourselves lines about how "everything is always OK because it is in God's hands." We must witness with our own being, in our own experience, the inspiration and guidance of the Divine that frees us from our issues. Otherwise, it will not translate to changes in our mental and emotional states.

Faith comes from knowing that God is providing us what we need in every moment. Our faith cannot be certain unless we are actually aware of this support. Faith is not blind. I hear people who are going through painful times say they guess they just have to trust. If you spend time with them, however, you will discover that what they are aware of and experiencing is only a difficult situation, not the presence of the Divine. They are using the idea of God to cover over their real feelings about what is happening. This quasi-faith keeps them from the real peace and inspired living that comes from honestly sharing their experiences of pain. Others place things in God's hands at the first sign of discomfort. They are unwilling to even feel or acknowledge what is bothering them, saying, "God will handle it." They say they have to accept whatever happens because, if they were not meant to suffer, they wouldn't be suffering, so there is no use in turning to the Divine. They forget that acceptance also includes accepting their own state. In their state of pain, they truly need guidance and support. Therefore, turning to God is real acceptance.

Body and Spirit

It is natural to lose sight of Divine care in difficult moments. As human beings, we are composed of two parts: spirit (our higher nature) and body (our lower nature). They don't always agree on the meanings of the painful events of our lives or how to respond to them. What we refer to as our self is a blend of body and spirit.

Our spirit is the breath of God that gives life to our bodies. It is referred to as the higher nature because it pertains to and draws its well-being from the Divine. Because our spirit is from God, meaning it is God's breath, it carries, aligns with, and displays the Divine qualities such as seeing, hearing, life, power, knowledge, love, and so forth. Without a spirit, our bodies are corpses with none of these qualities. The spirit is not dependent on things in the world for its well-being. It knows it is sufficed in every moment because it derives support and guidance from the Divine, which is without need. In each changing moment, our selves have the potential to experience the sufficiency that comes from relying on the support and guidance inherent in our spirit.

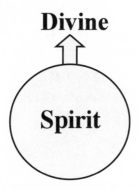

The Higher Nature

Our bodies are the vessel through which the qualities of our spirit are displayed. The body is referred to as the lower nature because it draws its well-being from things in the material world. When these things are taken away, the lower nature gets upset because it believes that losing these things threatens its well being. Rather than relying on the Divine for guidance, it resists these experiences and expends its energy on pushing away what is uncomfortable or trying to get things to go the way it would like. It desires the things and events that make it feel safe, comfortable, and stimulated. The body's sense of well-being is based most often in three areas:

- How we are treated
- What we get in the form of provision (money, health, relationships, possessions)
- Our position or role in life (whether we are strong or weak, leading or following, clear or uncertain, and so forth)

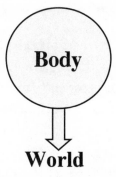

World

The Lower Nature

We have both the freedom of the spirit and the attachments of the body contained in one vessel, the self. Because the body and spirit have different natures, they are often at odds with each other. How we experience the difficult events of our lives depends on which part—body or spirit—is governing our awareness and guiding our perceptions in the moment.

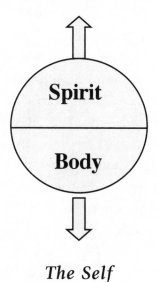

The Self

The Real Miracle

In life, we have experiences of both pleasure and pain. Some things please us; others do not. The lower nature wants what pleases it and resists the experiences that make it uncomfortable. The spirit does not make this distinction and moves forward, relying on the support and guidance of the Divine, regardless of what the world brings. If we follow our lower nature and act as if our well-being is based in things and events, we will think the answer to happiness is having certain things and living in a certain way. If we follow our spirit, we discover that happiness is the result of moving in harmony with the Divine, regardless of what we are given. When the lower nature is guiding our self, difficult events are seen as obstacles to fulfillment. The lower nature tells us balance and harmony are not available because what is happening is threatening what we draw our well-being from. This is how issues are created. In contrast, the higher nature turns to and follows Divine guidance in moments of difficulty. In this way, the events of our lives become catalysts of growth and positive change.

When the lower nature dominates our attention, our connection to spirit is eclipsed. Our well-being now falls into the hands of things and events. The self can only draw its well-being from one source at a time, either the world or the Divine through our spirits. When we draw from the world, we cut ourselves off from spiritual sustenance, that is, life, power, support, love, and knowledge. Thus, the self begins to starve. If the self is looking outside to the world for sustenance, it will begin to think the answer is more, that is, more goods, status, affection, recognition, or sensation. Regardless of how much of these things we get, it still feels as if something is missing.

We can never get enough of what we don't really need.

No amount of anything can take the place of Divine care and the ability to be at peace, regardless of what life brings. The pain or emptiness stays painful and empty when we chase things on the outside. The longer we stay in pain without being fed from our spirits, the less we participate in the Divine qualities. The things we think we need in order to be happy in fact keep us from the true happiness that is inherent in being. When we are looking for some miracle in life that will give us what we need, we miss the fact that life itself is the miracle. The question is, "Are we participating our not?" Are we moving forward and growing as individuals who rely on the guidance of God? Are we seeking certain comfortable familiar situations and avoiding pain?

I often ask the groups in our healing workshops, "How many of you have received the love and attention you wanted in life all the time exactly the way you wanted it?" I have never had anyone raise his or her hand. The bad news is that the world will disappoint us. The good news is that our well-being is not based on the world. Our well-being is in jeopardy only when we allow the feelings that tell us that it is to make our decisions for us. When we forget the Divine connection that is available through our spirits, our entire life swings in the balance of what happens to us because that is all we feel we have. None of us is in control of every aspect of the world. Living this way can create a very tense existence. When we believe our life is in the hands of what happens to us, we seek control and become frustrated when people, events, and even ourselves don't behave as they should. The poet Rumi says,

> *You cry that the world has hurt you*
> *You cry that the world has disappointed you*
> *But you do not cry that after all of this mistreatment you*
> *are still hopelessly and shamelessly attached to it.*

It is not bad to want things to be pleasing in life. It is natural and healthy to desire to be well, comfortable, safe, satisfied, loved, and appreciated. We can cause ourselves immense amounts of pain by pretending and living as if we do not need these things. However, these desires become a problem when they dominate our experience. The things of the world have a very fickle nature. They are always coming and going. We are up one moment and down the next. The things that bring us pleasure in one situation can be the source of great pain in another. Even our health and strength of body have a limited life span. Safety, happiness, fulfillment, and love are the by-products of living in harmony with God, not conditional scenarios to be chased after in a state of separation.

Because the lower nature is factory-installed equipment in each one of us, the journey of spiritual healing is moving from lower to higher nature and refining the self. Difficult situations are a part of life. How we respond to them determines whether we have a life of balance or one of separation and suffering. Acknowledging the painful experiences and issues generated by the lower self and accessing Divine guidance through our spirit is the crux of spiritual healing. Each time we reach out to the Divine, more of the qualities inherent in our spirits are displayed in our lives. The practice of remembrance does not cause Divine guidance to be there. Instead, it brings our awareness to the fact that it always is. When in remembrance, we are reminding ourselves of our spiritual nature and that in every moment, the Divine completely suffices us.

Self-Responsibility

When difficult situations occur in our lives, we draw guidance from either our higher or lower nature. Getting upset about what is happening in our lives is an indicator that we are listening to our lower nature and need to spend time in remembrance. Making the choice to be in remembrance can take humility and restraint. The foundation of our well-being depends on whether we are aware of God's support. Whether we are upset because of something someone did or did not do, what we got or didn't get, or what is happening with our health, the important thing is that we acknowledge that we are believing something unsupportive and need guidance. Usually, our immediate reaction is to try to fix or struggle against what is upsetting us because of what we believe the situation means. We try to change what is happening or figure out how to get what we would prefer without addressing our issues. In this way, the person seeking resolution is still operating from a sense of separation. We must say to ourselves, "Before I seek a solution or try to figure anything out, I must care for my heart that is hurting from following unsupportive issues.. Until my heart is experiencing spiritual sufficiency, nothing I do will lead to true resolution." In this way, we care for those parts of ourselves that are ready to grow and discover a new way of living. When we stop trying to change what is upsetting us, the pain we feel in our experience of a difficult situation becomes the call that brings forth the Divine response. We do not have to manufacture this call. It is inherent in the genuine need for guidance we feel in the pain of our unsupportive issues. Opening to the Divine is simply acknowledging this pain and the call within it while expecting a response.

One of my students once likened this process to buying or trading. When the difficult events of our lives generate an unsupportive issue, we can either buy what our lower nature is telling us, or trade it in for the guidance of the Divine. He joked that he always ends up with buyer's remorse when he follows his issues.

One of the most empowering understandings we can embrace is that our experiences of a situation are not fixed. They can change and are influenced by our orientation to higher or lower nature. Many people think of the self as static when it is actually always changing. Our self is essentially who we experience ourselves to be in the moment. As long as we believing unsupportive issues, the experience of what it is like to be us will not be positive. Our experience of a situation is like a pair of glasses or a filter through which we see the world and make decisions. As long as we see the world through the lens of our issues, we are not able to see the possibilities for harmony. When the lower self decides a situation means something painful for us, we will unwittingly choose and attract situations in our lives that fit with this experience. We then use this information as proof that the conclusions of our issues were correct. This creates a foundation of pain that affects all of our thoughts and beliefs.

Our responses to life, more than the situations we are given, determine if we feel balanced and fulfilled. Before moving forward into action, we must remove the glasses that tell us we are not whole and receive guidance from the Divine. When we are seeing clearly, free from the distortions of painful interpretations, the rest comes more easily. From fullness comes more fullness. First, we care for ourselves and open to the guidance and support that returns us to harmony. Then our actions lead will to peace and wholeness.

Reclaiming Wholeness

God is the one who created us. It is His job to care for us. It is our job not to take any other as our sustainer and turn to Divinity alone. Many of us suffer from role reversal. We think it is our job to care for ourselves and God's job to worship what we decide is good for us. We often keep ourselves stuck by asking the Divine how we can fix our problems while we are still following the guidance of our lower nature. Spiritual traditions tell us, "The Divine will not change a thing for you until you first change it inside for yourself."

When we admit that we are in pain and that what our lower nature believes about a situation is leading us away from what feels good, we change our focus within from lower nature to spirit. This is how we change a thing for ourselves. We then place our issues in the hands of the Divine which prepares us to receive Divine care.

The practice of remembrance tells us the Divine suffices us in every moment. Remembrance is not healing or dissolving the separation from what we need. Instead, it is dissolving the idea that we are separate. Only when we are willing to admit that our lower nature's point of view is bankrupt and surrender it for that of the Divine can we witness and experience genuine unity and sufficiency. This is such an important distinction. We are not turning to God fix our problems. We are turning to God to discover that our problems don't break us in the ways we believed they did and to respond to life from harmony. So many of us have been working for years to try to change things in our lives so that we no longer have to suffer, but we have not taken the time to see if our conclusions of suffering are even accurate. Acting as if our issues are true and then trying to heal them is like trying to scrub a shadow off the floor. We can scrub and scrub, but that shadow is not going anywhere until we shine light on it.

Ironically, the presence of a spirit within our selves makes the issues of the lower nature so unbearable. The spirit is uncomfortable in the prison of a self ruled by worldly attachments. If we did not have a spirit, there would be nothing within us to object to the life of the lower nature and reach out for more. The force within us that inspires us to change is the restless spirit with its innate capacity to participate in Divine harmony. This jewel within us can only take so much counterfeit currency before it demands the real thing. Many of the crises we face are really crises of spirit, manifesting in our health, relationships, and work life.

Receiving in Remembrance

When we are willing to acknowledge that we are in need of guidance and support, a transformation takes place. The events of life become the catalyst for our growth and a means for deepening our experience of happiness and fulfillment.

When something upsetting happens, it is important to be aware of what we are upset about. Illness, relationship struggles, and problems at work are all just words. It is important to become aware of what is upsetting us and weighing on our heart about these events. Each of us will be upset about these events for different reasons.

Being willing to name what is bothering us about a given situation will identify our problem. Once we have identified our problem, we can become aware of our experience and what our lower nature believes that problem means for us. This will identify our issue. Once we become conscious of our issues, we can evaluate whether or not they feel supportive. When we are honest about how our issues make us feel, it becomes obvious that they do not hold a very uplifting perspective. Developing the ability to discern whether or not our beliefs about a given situation are supportive is an essesntial skill. It allows us to see our beliefs as issues in need of support rather than something to base our lives on. Acknowledging that are issues are unsupportive is the step we need to take in order to be in a position to receive the Divine response.

Once we are in a position to receive, we begin our remembrance by repeating our name for the Most High. We are invoking Divine support and reminding ourselves of its availability. Now the active part on our end is over. We bring ourselves present and pay attention with every part of our being to what the Divine makes with our issues when we place them in caring Hands. We listen, but this listening is different than listening with our ears. It is listening with our experience. This means we look and feel through the lens of our experience by noticing what happens to our issues as we remember the name of God. The experience we feel inside is where the love and support are needed, so God responds to us in these places. The response may come in a feeling of calm, a sudden insight, a voice we hear inside or outside, a vision, or any other way. Each of us will receive a little differently. The important thing is that we are present and expect a response.

> One of my students reported, "When I turned to God in the beginning, I used to get a feeling that seemed to come with insight wrapped up in it. As I worked with listening more and more, I asked myself, 'If this feeling were a voice, what would it say?' Then I began to wonder, 'If it were a vision, what would if look like? What would it taste like, smell like, and on and on.' In this way, I involved all of my senses in listening. My connection and clarity then grew."

Relaxing our conscious minds creates space for guidance. When we place our issues in God's hands, we make room for new insights to reach us. In order to hear that guidance, we must stop talking and start listening. Many people are so busy saying, "Oh God, please take it away" or "Please show me what to do so I can get out of my experience," that they have not let go and made room for a response. We can make all the requests we want for healing, help, change, and intervention. It is right and good to remember that these things come from God, but, in the end, we must acknowledge our issues and listen.

> I had a student who was in a painful situation and kept saying repeatedly, "Oh God, please help me. I'll do anything."

While he was talking, what he was really saying was, "God, I don't want this experience. I want a different one. Show me how to make things the way I would like them to be." He was so busy sharing what he wanted that he forgot to listen for God's love and support regarding what he had.

Most of the time when people tell me that they are not receiving anything in remembrance it is because they are focused on their problems and not their issues. In times of pain it is easy to turn to the Divine as a way out. If we continue to act as if our issues are the whole truth and ask the Divine to heal them as if we are broken or change our situation, we will never discover true sufficiency. The Divine is not a palliative measure we turn to when we want to feel better. Rather we are seeking the guidance and support that will reveal a path of fullness in the midst of our struggles.

The way out of what hurts is discovering our spiritual sufficiency within it so we are able to move through what previously stopped us. Healing is an inside job. Opening to the Divine does not necessarily change the outside situation. It changes the individual who is in the situation. We see things differently, discover new inner strength and resources, and let go of the things that don't really matter. Through this change in our selves and the gifts of spirit, we realize true peace and sufficiency. Our actions align with the Divine, and we put forth beautiful responses rather than emotional reactions to the events of our lives. These responses go out in the form of beauty and create healing and wholeness in our lives. When this happens, we leave both the pain and the difficult situations far behind.

Caring for Your Self

When something happens that veils us from being aware that we are sufficed in the moment, it is easy to become caught up in our version of events and think this is the whole story. It is often our unwillingness to be present in that moment and reach out past our feelings and reactions to spirit that keeps us from knowing we are getting what we need to move forward in peace. Remembrance is reaching out to God past the borders of our experiential box and asking for guidance and support.

When we acknowledge the pain of our issues and turn to God, it is with the understanding that pain is one side of life and is not the result of some mistake. No one is at fault. We know that what is happening was meant to be because it happened. When walking in faith with God, we accept that each moment we are in is the right one for us. This is not a moral judgment. Simply, it is recognition that God guides us into greater realization of spirit through both seemingly positive and negative events. When we experience life as difficult, we seek God's support. When it is easy, we celebrate God's generosity rather than crediting ourselves. We see obstacles as necessary to the unfolding of our being and a means by which we can deepen our experience of the Divine. After all, we become who we are meant to be by walking the road that is laid before us.

Turning to the Divine in remembrance is an act of self-love. We are not trying to fix ourselves as if we are broken. Rather, we are acknowledging the pain of our issues with compassion when the difficult events of our lives cause us to feel as if we don't have what we need. When the conclusions of our issues are not supportive, even if we could win any argument or convince ourselves this is the way things are, we give ourselves time with Divine to receive the guidance we need.

If we take a moment to become conscious of what we look and feel like when we believe our painful issues, it becomes obvious that we are in need of support. The person who is under the sway of our issues is not the one we want making decisions and taking actions in our lives. The key to healing is caring for ourselves when we notice we are upset. No one can take this step for us. When we are in pain, we need to stop, and, rather than looking for some way out, take what is upsetting us and what we believe our situation means before God until the Divine reveals what we need to be at peace. Only then will our thoughts, beliefs, words, and actions be truly wholesome. I often use the analogy of a sponge. When wet, it is malleable and useful. When dry, it is hard, brittle, and not of much use. When we take the time to make sure we are soaked in the reality of God, we become stewards of our own hearts. This soaking changes us. We see, live, feel, and experience life differently. The situations, health, relationship, and career all going well are the natural results of our hearts being filled with this fullness.

It is said that God is found wherever we have a good opinion of Him. If we want to find the love and support of the Divine in a painful situation, we have to release all of the conclusions we have drawn that say, "If this is happening, God must be absent, cruel, uncaring, and so forth." Then we must reach out to the Merciful and Compassionate Divine. The person who is thinking these negative thoughts about the Divine is in pain and needs healing, so our suffering colors our conclusions. God carries the remedy for every pain. If we are weighed down, God is the Lifter of burdens. If we are trapped, God is the Bringer of freedom. If we are hurt, God is the Healer. If we are empty, God is the overflowing Nourisher. It goes on and on, but not always in the way the lower nature would demand. When remembering the presence of the Divine, we are turning to the most loving and beautiful reality we can conceive of. Restoring our good opinion of the Divine places our painful issues and experiences in the hands of the One who can heal and guide them.

Reliance

Every tradition tells us we are never given more than we can handle, but we must look inside to actually experience this as true. In spiritual healing, we have the advantage of knowing where we are headed, the experience of peace and sufficiency in the Divine. Although we know where we are headed, we have no idea of what we need to walk through or what it will look like when we get there. Knowing we are headed toward complete fulfillment, however, allows us to reach out to the Divine, regardless of what comes up inside of us, until we are at peace, and not stop with anything less.

The continuous Divine outpouring represents all of the love, support, strength, and insight we will ever need. Many of us live our lives as if there is something we must do to earn that support or believe it is only there in certain situations. The practice of remembrance reminds us that, in every situation, the hand of God is giving us what we need and brings our awareness to this presence.

It is said that, if we manage our affairs, God leaves us to

our management. If we surrender our affairs to God, then He becomes the manager. God does not say, "Complete yourself and then come to Me" He says, "Come to Me. I will complete you." The job of being human is not finished simply because we are alive. We must come into balance with all of the various elements of our lives before we reach the full potential of our humanity. No one reaches this state of peace through his or her own efforts. Rather, this peace is a gift of grace. We often act as if we should have our lives all together. However, we forget it is in our essential nature to need. We need air, food, water, and sunshine. Why should it be any different in our spiritual lives? Did we create ourselves? Do we know the complete purpose of life and everything that happens in it? Does anyone? Why try to do it on our own or look to others? It is in the difficult times when we are in pain that we are able to most clearly discover God's support. Giving ourselves time to be with God when we hurt ultimately fulfills the purpose of consciously experiencing the Divine in all aspects of our lives.

I saw this very clearly one afternoon with my newborn son. I was just getting out of a day of healing sessions when my wife handed me the baby. I played with him for a while. When I held him close to my wife, he let out this tremendous cry filled with need. My wife said, "Oh, my milk just let down." In that moment, I realized the relationship between need and love. My son had encountered the feeling of discomfort. Rather than try to figure out how not to feel it, why he was feeling it, or what he needed to do to make the feeling of need stop, he simply cried out in need, and the milk let down. He then nursed. Through the nursing, he grew until life brought him need again. Then he cried out again, nursed, and grew some more. It dawned on me that our relationship with the Divine is a lot like this.

Many spiritual traditions tell us, "When you call to the Divine, the Divine responds."

This simple phrase is the foundation on which spiritual healing is built. It is said that, when you turn to God for support, the Divine is happier to receive you than a mother who lost her son and thought he was dead only to have him returned to her, alive and well, after many years. In my years of being a healer, I have heard things from people about their past and seen people in situations that I wish never knew happened on this planet. No amount of anything I could say or do was going to make it all right. Something happens between a person and God that heals them in a way that is beyond what I can understand and can only feel incredibly grateful for. When we turn to God, we place our lives into Divine care. God's response to our turning is the healing power that changes lives. The answers and support that come from God help us in a way that we often did not even know to ask for and carry us into an experience we never knew was possible. God hears the deep prayers of what our hearts are truly longing for and brings these things to us in ways we did not expect. In spiritual healing, we open ourselves to the miraculous nature of God and accept the blessings of Divine response into our lives.

Those who experience this love say God is the most generous and complete lover they have ever known who brings healing in the true sense. Not only does he lead us to freedom, he also shows us that we were never really trapped. We only feel trapped when we believe the experiences that tell us we are not sufficed to be the whole truth and base our lives on them. When we struggle with events, we keep ourselves from the love, consideration, and time with our Creator that we need to straighten things out and learn what it means to be truly secure and content. Our spirit that allows us to remember and align with God's care in any situation is our greatest gift. Physical healing, happiness, and fulfillment are the natural by-products of moving forward with insight and revelation.

Chapter Summary

1. Many things happen that cause us to lose sight of Divine care.
2. As human beings, we contain both body and spirit, or higher and lower nature.
3. Problems are that what upsets us in our lives. Issues are what we tell ourselves these problems mean for us.
4. We care for our hearts by acknowledging our issues in a difficult situation and opening to Divine support.
5. We listen through the lens of our experience until we receive what we need to feel at peace.
6. This puts us into balance with the moment. We can then take actions that lead to more health and wholeness.
7. Each of us will receive guidance differently. The more we practice remembrance, the clearer our connection will become.

Exercise

Identify a situation that is troubling you in your life. What about that situation is bothering you? This identifies your problem. Now, take some time to notice your experience of this problem and what you believe this situation means for you that is so upsetting. This is your issue. How do you feel when you believe this issue is true? Turn in compassion to this place that is hurting, and acknowledge your need for Divine support and guidance. Begin remembrance, and place your issue in the hands of the Divine. Allow the response from the Divine to care for your issue. Do you notice what looks different about the situation after you receive this guidance? How might you respond differently?

Chapter Three

Breaking the
Cycle of Separation

You have all the ingredients inside for a nightmare.
Don't mix them
—Hafiz

As we have seen previously, the key to spiritual healing is facing what is upsetting us in our lives and discovering what we believe these upsetting situations mean for us. When we become aware of what a situation means to us, we can care for ourselves by taking time in remembrance. This allows us to receive the necessary support, guidance, and insight to respond to difficult events with harmony and heal. Too often, however, instead of acknowledging our experience, we resist what upsets us. This keeps us from becoming aware of our issues, and we live our lives from a foundation of separation. When we decide we have to live less than fulfilled because of something that is happening, our lives reflect this decision. The opposite of remembering is forgetting. If we forget a path of balance is always available to us, our selves cannot reach out for the support they need.

When following our lower nature, we begin to think there are reasons that bad things happen to us. Instead of realizing that difficult situations are one side of life, acknowledging our issues, and opening to support and guidance, our lower nature searches for reasons that explain why we are in this situation. These explanations are referred to as stories. They blame someone or something for our circumstances and act as if our life is in the hands of the world or events.

There are only two ways our stories explain why have problems. Something is wrong with us, or something is wrong with someone or something outside of us. In our stories, one of these two parties will always be at fault. The stories that the self guided by our lower nature come up with will always be tinged with pain and struggle because they are the explanations of a person who believes he or she must live in an unfulfilling way because of circumstances. Our stories don't make the pain go away. Instead, they explain why we are suffering and provide a focus for our emotional reactions. It is hard to acknowledge the pain of a difficult situation when we don't feel supported. If we forget the Divine guides us into a greater realization of our spirit through both seemingly positive and negative events, we have to make some sense of why these difficult circumstances are upon us. That is where our stories come in. Essentially, stories are the ways we try to soften the pain of our issues by focusing on our explanations of why we are in this situation. Instead of facing difficult situations and acknowledging we need support, they tell us we have problems and issues BECAUSE of someone or something. Stories are, in essence, the product of forgetting that every moment is in the hands of the Divine. Unfortunately, they distract us from our issues and keep us traveling down an unsupportive road.

I had a friend who was suffering from irritable bowel syndrome. I had lunch with him one day and asked how he was doing. He said not very well. When I asked what was bothering him, he said nothing he tried made any difference (problem). Through our discussion, we discovered that what he believed this meant for him was that he just had to learn to live with it (issue). Upon further discussion, we discovered he was telling himself he was in this situation "because he must not be doing something right" (story). His story explained both his continued sickness and why he was going to stay stuck, which lead to feelings of bitterness and made him very irritable. All of this added up to a sure recipe for staying sick.

The moment we create stories that explain why we are in a painful situation, we unwittingly cement that pain into our lives. Rather than acknowledging the pain of our issues and seeking support and guidance, we are busy explaining why we are in a unfulfilling situation. Once our struggles have a reason, they have a place in our experience. These explanations lock us into our painful experiences because not only do we believe the conclusions of our issues, but now we have explained to ourselves why things are this way. It is like a lock and key situation in which our stories are the jailor. Once we have our reasons why and are locked into our issues, we then take actions based in separation and have more to be upset about.

The Cycle of Separation

Our problems (what we are upset about), our issues (what we believe that upsetting situation means for us), our stories (our explanations of why these problems and issues are upon us), and the actions we take based on the combination of these three combine to create a cycle of separation. When we take actions based on our issues, rather than growing as people and moving forward, we get more of the original problem. Each time we go around this cycle, the spiral tightens, and our experience becomes more painful.

Cycle of Separation

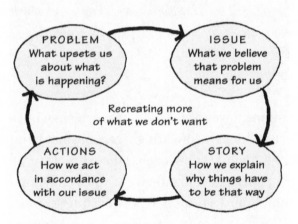

A cycle of separation can be created in the space of a moment. Usually, our issues and stories remain below the level of our conscious awareness. We don't wake up and decide, "Today, I am going to interpret the difficult events of my life in a way that is unfulfilling and lock myself into that pain by creating an explanation for why things are this way." Rather, they are instantaneously created by a self guided by the lower nature when events threaten the things we feel we need in order to be sufficed. We are alerted to the fact we are living in a cycle of separation when we are upset about what is happening.

Uncomfortable emotional reactions are the indicators that tell us we are in a cycle. These emotions are the driving force of our efforts to defend ourselves against what our issues tell us are unfulfilling situations. These efforts of defense are called resistance. The emotions of resistance are anger, sadness, and fear. Their many variations include frustration, terror, overwhelm, and depression. These emotions are how we feel about what is going on. They are our attempts at either pushing away what is unpleasant or chasing after what we would prefer.

It is natural to be upset about a situation that we believe forces us to live in an unfulfilling way. If it was true that we are not sufficed because of something that is happening and do not have what we need to respond in balance, than we should be upset. We should run, cry, fight, kick, scream, work hard, or do anything to get out of this situation and into one where we are OK. Without the guidance of the Divine these reactions can seem like our only alternative to suffering.

The Trap of Resistance and Stories

We can only live in a cycle of separation for so long before we begin to struggle against what is happening. It is unbearable to live without what we need and our resistance demands change. Resistance focuses on problems, and not issues, by struggling against what is upsetting us. It answers the question of why am I having a difficult experience with the answer, because such and such is—or is not—happening. In this way resistance overlooks our issues and fails to recognize our need for support. Acknowledging our issues and turning to God for guidance is called looking inside. When we believe that things or events dictate our responses and hold sway over our well-being, we look to the outside. We can point at them and say, "This is what is causing me to live in an unfulfilling way." Resistance believes that the answer to regaining harmony is to be found in changing what is upsetting us into what does not. Instead of turning to the Divine and opening to the support and guidance that can carry us through a difficult situation, resistance looks for some way to get out of what is happening. Because our stories identify what we believe is the reason we are in this situation, resistance focuses on these explanations. Now, the emphasis is on our problems and stories, but the self who is struggling to change what is upsetting us is the same one who decided we are less than sufficed. It is a lot like trying to get out of a hole with a shovel.

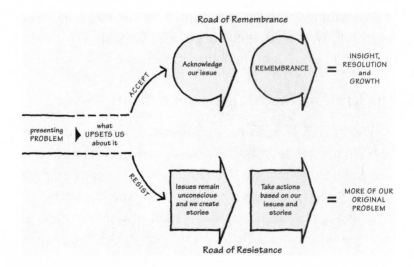

I had a client who was complaining about how tired she was feeling lately. She was unconsciously telling herself that this must mean she was getting old. Instead of acknowl-

edging that her self was telling her that she was getting old, which felt terrible, she decided she was tired because she had let herself go (story). She then focused on the explanation of her story by trying all kinds of diet therapies and supplements. They would work for a while, but she seemed to come back to the same feeling, which prompted her to try some new regimen. When we talked, I shared with her that as long as she believed that not being able to do what she used to do meant getting old, that was what she was going to get. As she acknowledged what her self was telling her and how horrible it made her feel, she realized she had long associated reaching a certain age with being old and useless because that was what she had seen in her family. As she turned in remembrance, the Divine revealed an exuberance inside of her that had nothing to do with age. She felt and realized many things and discovered a new sense of vitality.

Resistance or Remembrance

We can answer the questions of why I am in this predicament and what I have to struggle against if I want to get out of it in a split second, and we are off and running. These answers are the products of our own minds and serve as the basis for our story that separates us from the reality of spiritual subsistence. In these moments we are listening to our selves instead of the Divine.

Every painful situation is like a fork in the road. On the road of remembrance, when a difficult thing happens to us, we face what upsets us about it and become aware of what we believe this situation means for us. We then compassionately acknowledge these issues and place them in the hands of the

Divine for perspective and support. On the road of resistance, when a difficult thing happens to us, rather than face what is upsetting us and acknowledging what we believe as a result of it, we say, "No, I don't want this. I want something else." We then struggle against what is happening. Part of this struggle is explaining why we are in this situation, which distracts us from the pain of our issues. This creates a cycle of separation that will never lead to resolution because we have not healed the unsupportive issues that tell us we must live in a way that does not feel good. If we want to try to change our situation rather than looking inside to our issues, resistance looks outside and emotionally struggles with the explanations of our stories. In this case, the person who believes he or she is not sufficed is the person who is trying to make change.

I had a client who was very depressed and unhappy who did not feel she was in the right place in any aspect of her life. She felt she was in the wrong work, wrong city, and wrong relationship. Everything felt unfulfilling. Her lower self told her that meant she was just wasting her time and spinning her wheels. Believing this issue made her feel collapsed. It became hard to get out of bed in the morning. Her story told her that she was just spinning her wheels because she hadn't discovered her purpose in life. Rather than acknowledging her issue, she focused on her story and spent her time trying to find more meaning in her life. It is impossible for a person who has decided he or she is just spinning his or her wheels to find anything truly meaningful, so her efforts were unsuccessful. When she discovered her unconscious issue where she had decided she was just spinning her wheels and opened in remembrance, everything changed. She saw that her life was filled with opportunity and she was meant to enjoy it. Rather than waiting for the right situation to come to her, she realized it was in her hands to create a fulfilling life.

Anger, Sadness, and Fear

Our stories provide a focus for our emotional reactions by identifying why we are in a difficult situation. This allows us to try to change what is happening by channeling our emotions into tackling the explanations of our stories. Anger works through force or self-will, fear through avoidance, hiding and withdrawing, and sadness by despairing, complaining, and trying to attract intervention.

Most of our suffering does not come not from the events of life. Instead, it is from the meanings we attach to them. The ways that our emotional stories lead us to dealing with others and ourselves can be very painful because they are based in anger, sadness, or fear. The explanations of our stories, which tell us why we are in a painful situation, lead to feelings of unworthiness, judgment of ourselves and others, anxiety, pessimism, blame, defeatism, resignation, feeling like a victim or that we don't belong, and so forth. We then damage our lives and relationships with the actions we take based in these feelings.

The emotional solutions of our resistance will always require some form of effort before resolution can be found. I call this constructing hurdles in our healing process. We say, "I am in this situation that means something painful for me because of some reason (story). Until that reason is addressed, I will not be whole again." If our stories identify us as the cause of our problems, we have to contend with ourselves. If the world or some external force is the reason, we must contend with them before we can get out of this pain and have fulfillment. If we are the problem, when angry, we will try some variation of fixing or forcing ourselves to change. When fearful, we avoid certain situations and hide because we believe we are flawed in some way. If we are sad, we complain about our insufficiencies. If someone or something outside of us is the problem, we try to change them when angry, avoid them, and cut them out of our life when scared. We also complain about them and blame them for our unhappiness when we are sad about what is happening. All of these strategies are aimed at eliminating what we believe is the cause of our problems.

I had a client who came to me with chronic pain and exhaustion. When I talked to her about what really upset her about it, she shared with me that she felt like she was missing her life. This meant she was going to spend the rest of her life trying to push a rock uphill and never getting anywhere. Rather than acknowledging her issue and need for guidance, she was telling herself she was in this situation because she wasn't doing her life well enough. She had a whole list of things that she could be doing better. She could manage her time, set better priorities and boundaries, and so forth. Because this list was the reason she believed to be the cause of her struggle, she had been trying hard to balance these areas of her life. Unfortunately, the person who was trying to do better was the same person who decided her life was an uphill battle. All of her efforts carried this struggle. It was an exhausting process. Working on her story was causing her to be more tired, which, in turn, made it even harder to participate in her life. When she took time to acknowledge her issue and opened in remembrance, she realized that none of her life could be in balance until she was. The remembrance washed away many past memories that told her she needed to come last and she was not OK until everything was perfect. With this insight, for the first time in years, she felt a great sense of relief, freedom from pain, and relaxation.

Anything that explains to us why something difficult is happening and takes our attention away from our issues is a story. Some are prettier than others, but they are stories nonetheless. Even the belief that I am sick because I have some condition and what I am enduring is what happens to people with this condition can become a story. It keeps us out of the experience of what being sick means to us and places our awareness outside. This is contrasted, for example, with facing that the problem with being sick is we feel drained all the time. We then can become aware of our belief that tell us that being drained all the time means we are not going to make it. When we turn in remembrance with the feeling we are not going to make it, we receive what places us at peace with our moment rather than what explains why we have to feel bad.

People can become stuck in their stories and explanations of why. I have seen this very often in people with chronic problems. They cannot find resolution, so they continue to try one theory after another. "Maybe it's my diet...maybe it's my environment...maybe it's my relationship...maybe it's my heredity…" They continue to look for a reason for their problems, instead of facing them and acknowledging what they believe those problems mean for them while opening to the Divine.

Spiritual healing tells us that we are sufficed in every moment. If, however, we believe we are not sufficed because of events and take actions based in this belief, we will always feel as if there is something wrong. Until we realize the problem is within the issues of our own selves, we will continually be creating stories that explain why we are in this situation. It is the difference between realizing that our lens is out of focus and believing we need a new lens. The way to peace is peace. It is not trying hard and then finally being happy. It is achieving a state of balance that comes from receiving support and insight from the Divine, who is effortlessly in a state of balance.

Many times, I see people who are trying to trust, be loving, relax, be more responsible, listen, and so forth. They are following the stories that tell them they are in a painful situation because they don't do one of these things well enough. It takes so much effort because they are swimming upstream against their state of being that doesn't want to do any of these things. They really want to be upset because they are experiencing a situation that feels terrible and don't know what to do to make it better. No amount of effort will free us from our pain until the person who believes they are not sufficed opens to Divine support.

As long as we believe that a situation represents suffering for us, that is what we will get. I am not saying that difficult things do not happen in life. I am simply saying that what we tell ourselves about these things and the explanations we give for them often make what is happening worse. The struggles that result from our stories and emotional resistance do not have to be fixed or healed. They are the by-products of resistance and rapidly resolve when we discover our sufficiency in the Divine.

The Dilemma of Resistance

The definition of a dilemma is being in a situation with two bad choices. Following the road of resistance creates dilemmas. Dilemmas, in turn, create drama because we become sandwiched between accepting our issues and suffering or struggling to change what we believe is the cause of that suffering by tackling our stories. Until we remember that the guidance and support of the Divine are available to us in our moments of pain, we will be stuck with one of these choices.

No one in his or her right mind is going to quietly accept a life of suffering. Our only choice is to resist. Resistance tells us that, maybe if we fight or try hard enough, cry or complain loud enough, or run and scramble fast enough, we can change what we have decided is the reason we have problems.

Even if through our own efforts or the efforts of others we are able to change the circumstances that are affecting us, the person who was affected by them does not grow. The freedom from pain that we feel is still based in whether the situation stays a certain way or we take certain precautions. Many times people tell me that they feel fine as long as they do this and this and this and this. It requires so much effort because they have not grown to become the person who has the resources to move through the situation and finally become free from it. This allows our issues to remain unhealed inside of us, waiting and watching for the next similar situation to trigger the same feelings again. It is like climbing a mountain. As soon as you get to the top, another one is waiting after that.

Each time the efforts to change what we believe is causing our suffering don't bear fruit; we must come up with additional reasons that explain why these efforts didn't deliver. This adds another layer to our stories. The more layers we add, the less hope and faith we have that our efforts are going to change anything. This loss of hope is like a little death because we now have to accept that we are just not going to get what we need in this situation and we are left with our issues. It means we were unable to change the circumstances that we believed were causing our suffering, so we now just have to live in a way that is not fulfilling. Feeling as if we are doomed to live in an unsatisfactory way is unbearable. Regardless of how many times we have struggled and engaged in our stories unsuccessfully, we will always be willing to try one more time. It might not work, but at least it is not resignation. Besides, we think, "Maybe this time I will finally get it right."

The definition of insanity is doing
the same things and expecting different results.

We eventually begin to give up. When this happens, something breaks inside, and we go downhill very fast. I often see this decision as a dividing line between struggle and disease. This disease can happen with our bodies, relationships, or dreams. But, once we decide we are stuck with our issues, the results show up quickly and demonstratively in our lives. This decision is very different from acknowledging our pain in hope of Divine release. This is deciding that, because our efforts to address our stories have been fruitless, we are doomed to an unsatisfactory life, and leaving it at that. No one can bear the sentence of a life of suffering for long. The only thing that remains is escape and distraction. For some, it is drugs and alcohol. For others, it is shopping or food. For others still, it is television or medications. All of us have our favorites, but the point is that none of these escape strategies lead to resolution, and our lives become a pale shadow of our spirit's potential. They may provide relief in the moment, but they will not provide real movement or true and lasting satisfaction. That's why we will always need just a little more.

Taking Right Action

Spiritual healing does not teach us to sit idle and accept that life is filled with problems. Rather, the idea is not to respond to our challenges in a state of separation. When we believe we are not sufficed, the pain of the situation is on our own shoulders and is too much for us to bear. It is like asking directions from someone who is lost. How can someone who is hurt by a situation find a way to resolution on his or her own? Stories place our conscious minds in our explanation rather than looking at what we have decided a situation means to us, that is, our issues. We cannot move through or change what we are not in. As long as our stories distract us from our issues and experiences, we cannot discover sufficiency in the Divine and move forward. The issues and beliefs that contributed to our situation never get uncovered, and we don't grow as people. We can work on our stories from now until the end of time, and we will never really resolve them because they are the products of our own mind. Remembrance offers another alternative. It reminds us that, when we are in a situation in which we don't feel we have what we need and are believing something unsupportive, Divine guidance is always available to help us come back into clarity and balance.

Inherent in the pain of our issues is the feeling that something is not right. If it felt right, it would not be painful. This pain is asking us to reach out for something more. The pain tells us that our issues are not complete in the sense of wholeness and need the guidance and support of God in order to become balanced and harmonious. When we forget about Divine support, we don't gain the necessary insight to move forward through what is troubling us. We become trapped in our stories. Learning to uncover our unconscious issues and opening them to the guidance of the Divine frees us from the drama and dilemmas that are the products of a self-driven life and allows us to experience the fullness of our spiritual potential. Then our actions can lead us to a life of harmony and balance.

Chapter Summary

1. Refusing to acknowledge our issues is called resistance.
2. Resistance focuses on changing or avoiding the events that it believes is the cause of its discomfort.
3. When we are in resistance, we will always be experiencing some variation of anger, sadness, or fear.
4. Resistance drives us to create stories that explain why these negative events are happening and what we must do about it.
5. These stories lock us into a cycle of separation that lead to more of our original problem.
6. In our stories, someone or something will always be responsible for our suffering. The responsible party will be ourselves or someone or something outside of us.
7. Every painful situation is like a fork in the road. We can resist or remember.
8. The issues of our stories are self-created. Therefore, they do not need to be healed or transformed.

Exercise

Think about an upsetting situation in your life. Become conscious of any stories you are telling yourselves about why you are in this situation. Based on this story, what actions are you taking? If you stopped explaining why you are in this situation, what would you be left facing?

Chapter Four

Clearing Pictures
from the Past

When an inner situation is not made conscious,
it appears outside as fate.
—Carl Jung

Losing sight of what we tell ourselves painful situations
mean to us and getting caught up in our stories does more
than affect our present life. It colors our future as well. While
our conscious mind is engaged in our stories, our unconscious
is still very much present with the decisions we have made
based in our issues. Whatever we have decided a difficult situation means for us is what we get. Until we gain new insight
from our connection to the Divine our issues and stories
become like a lens through which we unconsciously interpret
future moments. These lenses carry all of the attached meanings
and associations of our cycles of separation. They only have
the ability to see what validates their point of view. Because
we have decided what a situation means to us in our unconscious, our minds screen out information that does not validate
its conclusion and focuses on the things that do. If the conclusions we have drawn are painful ones, the interpretations we
make about similar moments in the future will be painful as

well. Our habitual emotional resistance strategies kick in, and we act out our issues and stories one more time. When we are engaged in this way, we are not consciously available for new experiences and rehash the past. The longer we live as if our issues are true, the more proof we amass that they are. They become so familiar, and we align with them in so many ways that our choices soon lead to a life that mirrors our issues.

The issues held in the unconscious are like software programs we don't know we are running. We may not be conscious of them, but they are definitely affecting the operating system. Until they are made conscious through acknowledgement and opened to a spiritual second opinion, they remain unchallenged. If we have had an experience of being withheld from in an important relationship, which means we have to harden our hearts and not expect much from love, and this issue is explained by our stories that tell us we were withheld from because people only care for themselves or something is wrong with us, relationships start to look unattractive. Unconsciously, we have already decided we are in for an unfulfilling experience, so we go into a relationship with the brakes on.

When our issues are setting the landscape of our lives, it can seem like we relive the same pain over and over again. Unfortunately, the truth is that we have never left it. More accurately, we have never moved through it. We bring our unresolved past moment into every present moment and continue to experience it, align with it, and take actions that are based in our unresolved issues.

A friend of mine once shared that he realized he was always at the scene of the crime whenever difficult things happened.

This caused him to suspect that his struggles might have more to do with him than what was happening in his life. Many people change the cast and characters of their lives, but they continue to have the same type of experience. Looking through the lenses of our issues, we can turn anything with or without a heartbeat into being "just like my so-and-so" or feel like the same thing always happens, which has negative consequences for us. I like to call this God's merciless mercy. Wherever we go, there we are, and so are our issues. It can make us want to scream, and that's exactly what we need to do. A life lived from resistance will only increase in intensity until we stop, let go of trying to make things different, and place our issues in God's hands.

Many times, people are in remembrance without even being totally conscious that they are opening to the Divine. They only know that what they are doing is not working, and they acknowledge their need for help. When I later ask them where they thought that help was coming from, on reflection, they realize it was from some benevolent force. They were definitely sure that it wasn't going to come from them.

Pictures

You only need to read the newspapers to realize that horrible, tragic things happen every day to good people, innocent people, and even children. No one is exempt from challenges. These experiences vary in intensity, and each person has a different relationship to them. What is difficult for one person is paradise for another and vice versa. I have even worked with people who are struggling in life because they are receiving too many good things. Billions of people in the world would love that kind of problem.

Although the experiences vary in intensity and presentation, we are wounded by an experience when we say no to what is happening because of what we assume it means for us. We then either push away the experience or chase after what we would prefer. In spiritual healing, this is called stopping with pictures. The pictures are what life presents us in any given moment. Each instant is like a frame. Some of these frames are pleasing to the self. Some are painful. Each of these frames is replaced by the one that follows. It is then gone forever. Every moment is a new experience. Wounding is not the pain that happens from a difficult experience. Rather, it is the damage done by our issues, resistance, and stories. As long as our lives are based in painful issues, which are explain by stories, we remain engaged with the pain of that moment because we have not yet received the necessary support and guidance to move through it in harmony. In essence, the experience remains unresolved. This creates a negative feedback loop that keeps us locked in the pain of that moment. Part of our being stays engaged with the painful situation, and we play it out again in our lives because that is where we are unconsciously focusing our attention.

How many people do you know who are reliving the same painful experiences they had years ago? We can spend years trying to get over experiences when they were actually over long ago. We, however, have not resolved what that experience meant for us. We are without the insights and support we need to move forward in harmony. Resistance is like pushing the pause button on a movie, leaving the rest of the scene waiting

to be played. In doing so, we miss our chance to mature spiritually and limit our participation in all of our future moments.
We never experience the sufficiency of our spiritual connection or our ability to move forward in a new way. Our lives
then become transfixed around this developmental stopping
point. We then repeatedly relive the same experience with
different players. Without our Divine connection in these
painful moments, we do not have any choice except stopping.
We are unable to go through this picture because who we are
attached to being simply does not have the resources to respond
with harmony.

One of my favorite one-liners is, "If you find yourself going
through hell, don't stop." This is so important because where
we stop is where we stay. If we say no to an experience that
feels like hell because of what it means to us, our consciousness
stops there. Suffering begins with no. Whatever we say no to in
an experience is what we will get more of.

What we resist, persists.

I often refer to spiritual healing as a path of yes. We say yes
to what is upsetting us. We say yes to what it means to us. We
say yes to the fact that we need guidance. We say yes to Divine
support. We say yes to what comes to us from the Divine. We
say yes to how that changes us. If we say no at any of these
points, we stop the process.

The strangest thing about resistance is that we resist experiences that have already happened. We have already taken the
blow. The damage is done. If we don't acknowledge this and
allow God to put the pieces back together by revealing our spir-

itual sufficiency, we cannot move forward in balance.

> *I had a student who was sharing what she had learned about her heart in a three-day workshop we had presented. She said she had learned that the world could break her heart. She went on to say, however, that she had discovered a connection to the Divine that could put it back together better than before and in a way she never imagined possible.*

Baggage

Our cycles of separation and pictures are the baggage we bring into an experience. When we get upset about something that is now happening in our lives, it is usually carrying the weight of these stored experiences. We are often not upset for the reasons we think, or the incidents of today are bringing up the pain of our past. Usually, our stories, issues, and attachments remain behind the scenes in the unconscious setting the tone for our lives. The ways we are living out of harmony often go unnoticed until something happens that is painful enough to get our attention. Then we have a problem.

We can discover the issues we carry inside by paying attention to who we become when things go wrong. Adversity introduces us to ourselves and helps us uncover the issues and stories that are at the foundation of our struggles. Noticing how we react to painful circumstances will give us insight into the behaviors and beliefs that contributed to our situation. Difficult moments reveal the unconscious issues and personas that are next in line to be released in order to make space for more fullness. We only need to look as far as our own lives to find the next step on our spiritual path.

CLEARING PICTURES FROM THE PAST

Cleaning the Past

Usually, when we turn in remembrance with an issue, we will realize that this is not the first time we have felt this way. A troubling situation in the present can trigger unresolved issues from the past. We stopped with the pain of the situation then, and we still don't have what we need to move through these situations today. The combination of our stopping with the pain of the past and the damaging effects of listening to our stories are most likely contributing to our present difficulty. This doesn't mean we are carrying some baggage from the past every time we are hurting. However, if we are taking a situation personally, are more emotional than the situation allows, or are responding in a habitual way, the cycles and pictures of our past are probably influencing our experience. The present challenge represents a chance to free our selves from these unresolved issues and come into a fuller experience of the Divine.

I had a client who was suffering from a swollen prostate, incontinence, and painful urination. It upset him that he never knew when the next embarrassing or painful moment was going to hit. This caused him to feel as if he always had to be on his guard. As he acknowledged this feeling, he realized he had been feeling this way since he was very young. He had grown up in a violent household. On top of that, he had been bullied as a young child. As he acknowledged this place that felt as if he could never relax and opened in remembrance, a sense of relief washed over him. He felt a deep strength within himself and knew that, whatever came his way, he would be supported in facing it. Not only did his prostate and urinary difficulty resolve, but also years of fear and tension were removed by facing his challenge in remembrance.

We don't have to go digging around in our unconscious to find the pictures and issues that are affecting us today. They will make themselves known to us when we face the problems of our lives. We only need to pay attention to what comes up for us when we move in the direction of freedom. When we begin to receive Divine insight and support in a painful experience, all of the past pictures associated with this experience will surface when they feel this healing energy. These pictures come up because they feel the possibility for resolution. The issues from our past also need acknowledgement and time with the Divine connection to get what they need in order to heal. Discovering our sufficiency in the Divine breaks these pictures and shatters the lenses through which we were painfully interpreting our moments. This releases us from our cycles of separation and allows our lives to come into balance.

When the doors of perception are cleaned,
we will see things as they are; infinite.
William Blake

What Hit You Could Not Have Missed You

Usually, instead of facing the painful events of our lives and allowing the moment to reveal what we are ready to release, we want to know what we need to do in order to make things better. We act as if what is happening is just an accident that we have to get around. We believe that, if we can somehow make things better, our troubles would all go away. We forget the events of our lives are the raw material for spiritual growth and life is not about things going right. It is about growing as individuals and discovering new, more fulfilling ways of living. Mystics tell us, "What hit you could not have missed you."

Our painful experiences carve out and create the vessels that hold the water of Divine response. In these moments of need, we are open enough to receive what is beyond the self's resources to come up with. So many people come to our workshops with "how" questions. How can I live without being stressed? How can I be more loving? How can I not feel so bad? How do I get along with my spouse?

I remind them that the way out is through. If you are stressed, unhappy, in pain, or arguing, face the pain of these situations with the help and support of your spiritual connection. When you are on the other side, you will know how. We must be willing to be human, get emotional, and feel our own weaknesses. From there, we can be aware of our need for revelation and open to spirit for support.

One day, I realized I was only half-paying attention to my daughter and felt like I was missing her growing up. I immediately began resolving to be more present with her. Instead of facing my problem that I felt like I was missing her growing up and acknowledging my issue, I instantly began working toward being more present with her, which was the opposite of what was causing me pain. It was one more resolution on a large pile of resolutions of things I needed to do better. As I noticed this, I faced what was upsetting me and realized I was telling myself that she was slipping away. As I turned in remembrance to God, I was shown how we were of one heart and losing her was impossible. With this newfound insight and experience of being inextricably connected, I discovered that being present with her was second nature. The grace of God can accomplish things with one insight that all of my resolutions to be a better father put together cannot begin to touch.

The Heart's Compass

The pain and struggle we experience from resistance is not a punishment for doing something wrong. Like sidelines on a soccer field, these struggles are in our lives to tell us that we are going in the wrong direction. Struggle tell us the actions and thoughts we are having are out of bounds from what is healthy and balanced for us and we need to turn around and go another way. The circumstances of our lives trouble us to the point that we must acknowledge our need for guidance and support. In this way, through Divine revelation and insight, more of the vastness of our spirit is displayed in our experience, and our humanity is beautified.

Each of us is unique. None of us is born with an instruction manual telling us exactly what is right for us in every situation, but we have been given a heart. That heart has been blessed with the ability to tell truth from falsehood. It is comfortable with the truth and uncomfortable with falsehood. The gift of this is that our experience will always be uncomfortable when we are following our lower nature and believing we are not sufficed. Our hearts can then act like a compass that point in the direction of what fulfills us.

By acknowledging the issues that make us feel uncomfortable and turning to God, we trade our objections and stories about what is happening for God's support and guidance. We say to God, "I may think that what is happening is wrong and terrible, but, rather than resist and try to get what I want, I acknowledge my experience and what I am telling myself about this situation. I place my issues in Your hands and open to Your guidance and support trusting You to reveal what puts me at peace."

Many times we are living our lives not to hurt and have forgotten how much fullness there is to find. There is no end to the depth of fullness we can experience because there is no end to the Divine. The problems in our lives are asking us to release the things that are in the way of receiving this fullness. Every realization and identity has a shelf life of one moment. After that, it begins to become stale. We are constantly trading yesterday's me for today's new creation. If instead, we resist a painful experience, we will stay right there in pain, creating painful stories that explain why these things are happening. Rather than living a life of resistance, spiritual healing allows us to trade in the issues that never made us feel good in the first place.

The Physiological Cost of Resistance

The moment we explain why something is happening to us, it has a spot in our lives. In that moment, we begin to suffer its effects. Statistics tell us that 70 percent of all hospital visits are stress-related. Stress is a manifestation of chronically unresolved situations and issues. The combination of unresolved emotional states and the poor choices we make because of our stories quickly leads to illness on many levels. This can show up in our bodies, relationships, or lives, but the damage becomes evident somewhere. Living our life in resistance leads to illness and breakdown in three ways:

1. When we resist our problems, we step out of the flow of life. Resistance does not get us out of our problems and issues. They just place our conscious mind and energy in a different direction. Meanwhile we are in pain about what is happening doing things that don't truly feel supportive. It takes incredible levels of energy and tension to deny ourselves an experience. When we decide a situation means we must live without what we need, this taxes our physiology in numerous ways because we must live with the results of our decision. Living in resistance creates an environment of stress, burdens our immune systems, and brings about distress. Consequently, the chemical messengers of distress—cortisol, adrenaline, and insulin—increase. These physiological responses to distress throw off the delicate pH balance within our systems because they increase overall acidity. Our cellular machinery is designed to work best within a narrow, slightly alkaline range of 7.35 to 7.55. With even a slight excess acid load, efficiency of energy production in our cells is decreased. There is also a loss of resilience to infection, viruses, and disease, and the ability of our cells to repair themselves is compromised. All of this contributes to fatigue, illness, and pain.

2. Stories and our roles in them cement us into emotional states and keep us locked into a detrimental cycle. Our emotional states have incredible influence over our physiology. They are in direct communication with our bodies, and they are the inter-

face between our thoughts/perceptions and physiological responses. If our minds judge an experience to be a bad one, that must be resisted, it sends chemical signals to the body that bring about emotional states of being. When we resist our problems and become engaged in our stories, these emotional states become chronic because we never move through these experiences and we continue to feel the same way about them. If we are angry, our bodies become tense. If we are sad, they become dense. If we are fearful, they become agitated and hyper aroused.

If we are chronically angry, we tend to get diseases related to tension. Hypertonicity leads to cramping, knotting, and toxic buildup in the muscles and tissues of our bodies. Over time, this can cause fibrosis, tissue degradation, and inflammation. Right now, there is a tremendous amount of research being done on the effects of long-term tension and its relationship to inflammation. Chronic inflammation has been labeled as a key contributor to many disease states such as heart disease, diabetes, Chron's disease, arthritis, fibromyalgia, migraines, and constipation.

If we are chronically sad or depressed, we have a tendency toward diseases of excess. When we are depressed, we have poor respiration and circulatory response and are less likely to exercise or make conscious food and lifestyle choices. This leads to excess or congestion of body fluids, obesity, asthma, and general system wide depression.

3. When we are chronically afraid or worried, we open ourselves to diseases of over stimulation. Constant agitation leads to the exhaustion of the body's resources and an inability to get enough nutrients and support. Our parasympathetic nervous systems are engaged in a constant state of fight or

flight, which engages the hypothalamus, pituitary, and adrenal glands in production of hormones that raise our blood pressure and heart rate. Over time, this leads to chronic hyperarousal, high blood pressure, arrhythmias, sleep disorders, chronic headaches, backaches, anxiety, and a host of other disorders. All of these factors compromise our overall system integrity.

When we live according to our stories, resolution is always one more step away. Constantly chasing relief is disheartening, and our bodies soon become exhausted. Then they become worn down and finally stop working. We literally become sick and tired of being sick and tired. Not only are we carrying more than we can handle, but the beliefs and actions based in our stories are often not healthy or in balance with what is right for us, which further complicates our situation. The loss of heart that comes from being unable to resolve what is troubling us is perhaps the most damaging element of all.

The body must be nourished physically, emotionally,
and spiritually. We are spiritually starved in this culture.
Not underfed, but undernourished.
Carol Hornig

All of the factors mentioned previously weaken our natural defenses and impair our body's innate ability to heal itself. The combination of the physical stress associated with resistance, chronic emotional states, and the poor choices we make from our stories leads to an environment of breakdown. In this day and age of ever-increasing toxic exposure and global travel, our systems need to be functioning at optimal levels to avoid being compromised.

Whatever we are thinking to ourselves when we are angry, sad, or scared inside is part of our cycle of separation. The issues of unworthiness, self-hatred, stress, burnout, depression, hopelessness, depletion, tension, excess, and their corresponding illnesses are all the fruits of an emotional self-driven life. These issues rapidly resolve themselves, and the body heals quickly when we face what is really troubling us. Through Divine guidance, we can free our selves from the painful cycle of repeatedly injuring ourselves with our issues and stories.

A client of mine was having all kinds of back and knee problems. She was upset because she was beginning to feel like a cripple (problem). Not being able to manage things meant she was going to be a burden to other people (issue). Rather than acknowledging this issue, she followed her anger that told her she was in this situation because she was so weak (story). This led her to believe that she had push harder and crack down on herself. In this paradigm, she felt like a burden. Instead of acknowledging the pain of that belief, she fought against it with her personal strength, which created incredible tension in her lower back. Living this way was literally bringing her to her knees as her body began to quickly deteriorate under the strain. As she acknowledged her feeling of being a burden, she discovered this was not the first time she felt useless and dependent. Her back and knee pain was bringing up many feelings from her past that had been stuffed. As she turned in remembrance to the Divine, she discovered a resource that was there for her in a way she never knew. She realized she was loved. Like everyone else, she needed to be occasionally supported. This washed away the stories from her past as she traded in her issues for Divine support. She felt carried, and her back pain soon resolved itself without the constant assault of angry tension.

Whatever problems result from resistance are not really problems. Rather, they are ineffective attempts at management. They are simply the result of turning from divine care based on resisting situations that we judge to be negative. No event in life can irreparably harm us because our well-being is not based in events. It is based in spirit. Every moment provides us the opportunity to turn to one or the other. When we listen to the lower nature instead of spirit, the real suffering begins. The world can mistreat us, take things away, and even put us in terrible positions, but it cannot ultimately harm us unless we live as if our well-being is in its hands. Real freedom does not come from getting what we want. It comes as a result of realizing the love and support of God in both positive and negative experiences. Behind both is the hand of God guiding us into uncovering and realizing the nature of our spirit. Spiritual healing focuses on moving us through painful situations with the support and guidance of the Divine and undoing the damage of our issues and stories. When both of these things are accomplished, healing happens, and balance is naturally restored.

Chapter Summary

1. Wounding is the result of denying ourselves an experience.
2. When we deny ourselves an experience, we stay stuck at that developmental stopping point.
3. The moment we stopped with becomes frozen in our consciousness. It is called a picture.
4. We now see and interpret life through the lens of that picture.
5. Our cycles and pictures become linked so that, whenever we experience a similar situation to our pictures, our cycles engage, and we get more of the same.
6. Noticing how we respond to painful situations will reveal our cycles and pictures to our conscious mind.
7. When we acknowledge our present issues, pictures from our past will often surface to be healed.
8. Resistance and our cycles of separation create physiological distress and can lead to disease on many levels.

Exercise

Think about a situation that is troubling you today. Face what is bothering you about it, and become conscious of what you are telling yourself this situation means for you. Have you ever felt this way before? What were the circumstances that caused you to reach that conclusion? Take some time in remembrance, and see what the Divine has to share with you about these past experiences.

Chapter Five

Realizing Emotional Freedom

If you want to be happy, put your effort
into controlling the sail, not the wind

To get out of resistance, we must start with becoming conscious of the times we are in it. It begins with realizing that we are upset about something that is happening in our lives and taking the time to face it. Very often, we are so caught up in our stories explaining why we are in pain and trying to change what is happening that we may not even notice we are upset. Whatever we are thinking to ourselves when we are angry, sad, or scared is part of our cycle. By noticing we are emotional, we can avoid spinning in our stories and get to the issues inside that need Divine guidance.

One of the most common places I see people being stuck in their process is how they deal with their emotions. Many people misunderstand their emotional states as problems that need to be fixed or controlled. They believe that getting upset is a character flaw and work on their anger, sadness, or fear as if they are the problem. It is impossible to be anything except upset by a situation when we believe it means we must live without what we need. Upset emotions let us know that we are carrying issues that need support and guidance.

Our emotions only become a problem when we allow them to guide our actions. Too often, we ignore or stuff our emotions and do not admit to ourselves that we are angry, sad, or even scared about the way things are going. By now, most of us have realized that acting on our emotions often complicates the situation. That is why they are judged and controlled so often. The key is feeling our emotions without having to act on them. We only need to be aware of them long enough to find out what we are upset about. Without emotional self-honesty, we lose our connection to the upsetting problem. If we are not in relationship with our problems, we cannot discover the issues that need support. When we embrace our emotions as allies, they focus our awareness. Emotions are like fingers that point to what we are resisting and bring us into relationship with our problems. They point by showing us what we are upset about in the following way:

- We are angry about ...what?
- We are sad about...what?
- We are afraid of...what?

Facing what we are upset about is called walking through our emotions. If we do not take time to become aware of what we are upset about, we are often passed around from emotion to emotion. In each one, we are trying a different strategy to change whatever is happening that is upsetting us. We will often vacillate between the three emotions of anger, sadness, and fear, but none will lead to resolution because our issues have not been addressed. I often hear things like, "I was afraid of making mistakes for so long that I started to get angry with myself for being scared all of the time. Not liking myself became depressing, and I felt sad because I can't seem to get myself together. This made me afraid of trying and I began to withdraw. This made me even angrier at myself because I wasn't even trying."

The longer our upset emotions run our lives, the longer we go without what we need. Facing what we are upset about and the reason it is painful for us begins the process of spiritual transformation.

I had a client who came to me for healing because she felt like she was too angry. Acting on this anger had caused many problems in her life. She had become very depressed and even suicidal. Her anger had led to sadness and eventually to fear, which made getting out look attractive. I told her that getting angry was not the problem. In fact, not enough people are letting themselves feel angry about what is going on in the world. As we worked, I helped her to see that the anger was not the problem. Rather it was letting her anger run the show that was causing her pain. We discovered she was angry about the fact that nobody seemed to care. She felt she was not supported and there was too much for her to handle. As she acknowledged this issue and stayed in remembrance, she started to receive Divine care. As this and other pictures cleared, she realized she had the support of God. The pieces that were hers to carry felt manageable. She released her issues and stepped forward, feeling supported by God. She was then able to do her part to heal injustice without feeling overburdened. She continues to act in alignment with the Divine and has helped many people heal from the pain of traumatic situations.

A Cycle of Emotions

There is a distinct relationship between the cycle of separation and the emotions of anger, sadness, and fear. Each of us feels all three of these emotions but in different ways. One of these emotions of resistance will be associated with each stage of our cycles of separation. We will be angry, sad, or scared about what is upsetting us (our problems). We will draw angry, sad, or fearful conclusions about what these events mean for us (our issues). Finally, we will explain why we are in this situation with angry, sad, or fearful stories.

Cycle of Emotions

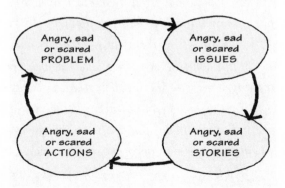

All of us have habitual patterns of responding to the difficult events of our lives. While some of us get angry about what is happening, another person will be sad or afraid of the same situation. While one person can have angry issues based on what they are upset about, the next person has sad ones. This is referred to as our emotional constitution. Where these emotions show up in the cycle of separation has a lot to do with what emotions were acceptable and expressed in our families of origin. We incorporate the emotions that worked for us in getting what we wanted and the ones we saw used to rationalize unbalanced behavior.

When we understand where in the cycle of separation we habitually feel which emotion, we can move through the challenges of our lives more quickly. By understanding that, whenever I am upset about something I am actually sad about what is going on, I can cut through all my mental chatter and face what I am sad about. Because I know that my issues are always based in fear, when facing what I am sad about, I simply must ask myself, what fearful conclusions and decisions am I making based on what is upsetting me. ?" By being aware that I explain my issues with angry stories, I realize that, when I am angry, I am trying to explain the reason why I am sad and must respond in a fearful way. Gaining awareness of how our emotions are moving us around the cycle of separation allows us to more quickly face what upsets us, acknowledge our issues, and avoid becoming caught in our stories. The more we understand how we react to the painful events of our lives, the easier it is to recognize them as just that, reactions, and turn from our cycles to the Divine in remembrance.

Understanding Our Cycles

We can become fixated on any aspect of our cycle. While we sometimes express the emotions associated with our problems, the emotions of our issues and stories are driving our expression other times. Usually, we are most familiar with the emotions of our issues because they are how we have decided to respond. Next in familiarity are the emotions associated with our stories. In most cases, we are least aware of the emotions of our problems. We are least aware of our problem emotions because feeling them leads to facing what is upsetting us. That is the last thing resistance wants to do.

To understand what emotions we feel in each stage of the cycle, we must become aware of our reactions. We ask ourselves, "How do I feel when difficult things happen?" There is a difference between what we feel when we actually face the fact that something difficult is happening and the emotions we feel about what is not happening. It is the difference between saying, "I am really sad because I wanted this relationship to work. And, acknowledging that it makes me angry when I have to face the fact that it didn't."

Once we know which emotion is associated with our problems, we move on to discovering the emotions of our issues. The emotions associated with our issues can be subtler than those of our problems. To discover which emotion is associated with our issues, we become aware of what we are feeling when deciding what a situation means to us. We ask ourselves, "Is the person who is deciding what this situation means angry, sad, or scared? What is the emotional flavor, direction, or bent of my issues?"

Finally, after we are clear on our issues, we look to our stories. We notice which emotion is associated with the stories that tell us why we are in difficult situations. Are we angry, sad, or scared when explaining why? Do our stories sound like the explanations of an angry, sad, or scared person?

Our problems, issues, and stories combine to create our cycle of separation. Our problems lead to issues, which lead to stories, which lead to actions that get us more of our original problems. Our emotions mirror this process in the same way. For instance, if our emotional makeup is angry, sad, and scared, we will be angry about what is happening, decide it means something sad for us, and explain it with a fearful reason. We then take an action that causes us to have more to be angry about.

> *I worked with a client who was angry because he felt like a coworker was always telling him what to do (problem). This made him feel inconsequential and meant he was just a lackey, which felt sad (issue). He explained this situation with a story that said things were like this because he didn't have as much experience as the other person, which felt frightening, and led him to just going along with whatever his coworker said when push came to shove. This only gave him more to be angry about. When he acknowledged his issue of feeling inconsequential and having to be a lackey in remembrance, he saw he was on equal footing with his partner. He realized there was room enough for both of them to create side by side. This was what his heart was really longing for. Rather than getting angry at his colleague or leaving, he was then able to create a dynamic and fulfilling relationship.*

Walking Through Our Emotions

We usually don't spend much time being aware of our emotional states. We may be upset by something and not be conscious of what we are upset about. Learning to identify when we are upset and allowing that emotion to guide us into relationship with what we are upset about is an essential skill. Often, when we are upset, we want to know why we are upset without having to really feel the emotion. Being upset doesn't feel good. It is easy to see it as a shortcoming on our part. We say things like, "I don't know why I am acting this way or what is wrong with me today." The only way to find out what we are upset about is to feel the emotion and let it show us. We cannot discover our problem by wondering what it might be as if it is a process we are not connected to. Part of being human is becoming emotional. Each of us has emotions that we don't like to feel. Some of us don't like to be angry. While others don't like to admit we are scared, others judge and avoid the feeling of sadness. As long as we view these emotions as taboo, we separate ourselves from the ability to identify our problem, discover our issues, and receive Divine support. When these emotions are owned and moved through in a process of remembrance, we discover vast amounts of life force and freedom that avoiding these emotions was cutting out of our lives.

Physiological Signs

Whenever we are in a resistance-based emotional state, our body will exhibit the signs. We will feel physical sensations in our body that are caused by the emotion that is being held in that area. Think of the last time you were really angry. Did you become tense? When you are sad, do you feel weighed down? This is the effect of these emotions on our bodies. Our bodies will often break down in the exact location where these chronic emotions are stored. If we learn to pay attention to the sensations of our bodies, they will let us know when we are emotional and resisting something. This means we will spend less time in our cycles and more time receiving what we really need. Whenever we feel the sensations of tension, being weighed down, butterflies in our stomachs, or any other discomfort, we stop and ask ourselves, "What emotion is causing this sensation? When we are not sure which emotion is causing the discomfort, we can exaggerate the sensation by allowing our entire body to mimic the sensation, like we are playing charades. Noticing what we feel in this exaggerated position will help us identify the emotion.

> *I once had a client who was having difficulty with an employee at work. She could not figure out why the relationship was not going well. I asked her what her body felt like when she brought this person to mind. She immediately began to get a headache. I asked her what the headache felt like. She said it felt a volcano that was about to explode. I then asked her what emotion was in that volcano. She said anger. When I asked what she was angry about, she said that this person was never satisfied. This meant she had to go around and around with this person on every single thing and waste her valuable time on something that would go nowhere. When she realized her issue and turned to her remembrance practice, she received the insight and support she needed to grow and handle this situation. Her emotion literally pointed to the exact problem of this employee who was never satisfied that she was avoiding and helped her discover and move through an issue that was affecting her work life.*

The beauty of our bodies is that they are very straightforward with us. When something is bothering us, they clearly let us know in the form of uncomfortable sensations. These sensations let us know we are emotional about something, which lets us know we are resisting and whatever we are thinking is not going to lead us in the direction of healing.

Uncomfortable sensations are caused by an emotion that points to a problem. Behind which is an issue that needs acknowledgment and Divine support so we can free our spirits from the influence of the lower nature and become the person who has the resources to deal with what is happening from harmony.

If what we are thinking is causing us to feel uncomfortable anywhere in our body or if we are feeling sensations of uneasiness, being burdened, or tension while we are thinking about our lives, then we are emotional about something. This tells us that we need to stop what we are doing and spend time in remembrance until we feel at peace. How many times do we really stop and ask ourselves how it feels to think the thoughts we are thinking? How many times do we notice whether our thoughts are based in pain and emotional reaction or peace? I see people very sincerely trying to change their lives, but they have not answered this question. Peace will lead to more peace and reaction to more things to react about.

Usually, when someone is not sure how to deal with a situation, it is because they are upset by it but don't want to act that way. Many times people ask me how to respond to different situations in their lives, especially their relationships. They want to know what they need to do differently so they don't keep getting what is upsetting them. Before answering them, I first ask them how they feel about what is going on. If they are upset, there is no answer to the question of how to handle the situation. Until they are at peace with the moment, they have not become the person who can take actions that lead to harmony. Clarity comes first, and action follows. It isn't the other way around.

Many times, I hear the message that this process would take too much time. People feel that, if we were conscious of every time we felt uncomfortable and took the time to reflect upon those feelings with God, we would never get anything done. This process only seems like a good use of our time when we reflect on how much energy is spent having to make up for the things we do from uncomfortable states of being. Our experience of a situation must become first on our priority list. When how we are doing inside becomes more important than what is happening or what needs to be done, our lives come into balance because we begin to do the right thing at the right time. Doing the right thing at the right time is the essence of being in harmony.

The Door Swings Both Ways

Emotions are like a door that swings in two directions. One way leads to our explanations and stories. The other leads to the problem that is troubling us. It boils down to a yes or no response to the events of our lives. Do we say yes and face what we are upset about? Or, do we say no and begin to resist? Once we realize what we are upset about, we can acknowledge our issues and receive healing and guidance from the remembrance. When we go through the door of yes, the entire emotional complex of our cycles unravel as our stopping with pictures is replaced with walking through what hurts with God. In this process, we stop listening to ourselves and place our lives in the hands of the Divine. We no longer hurt ourselves with our stories, and the tension associated with resisting the moment drains away. Making this switch from resistance to remembrance places our emotional bodies in a state of peace as we realize our sufficiency in spirit. This peace is passed onto our bodies. It is no secret that, when we are in a state of peace, our bodies heal faster, our relationships thrive, and our lives work better.

Chapter Summary

1. Getting out of resistance starts with noticing when we are upset about something.
2. Whatever we are thinking to ourselves when we are upset is part of our cycle.
3. Each of us has an emotional constitution that relates to the cycle of separation.
4. Understanding our emotional constitution helps us disengage from our reactions and cycles and more quickly turn in remembrance.
5. Emotions are like fingers that point to what is bothering us and lead us to the situations we need to face.
6. Our bodies will always display the resistance of our emotional states in the form of uncomfortable sensations.
7. The feelings of discomfort in our bodies are caused by an emotion that points to the problem that we need to face to discover and heal our issues in Remembrance.

Exercise

Each of us resists the painful events of life in different ways. Learning to recognize what you feel like when you are in resistance can help you catch yourself and surrender earlier and more often. Think about something in your life that is not going the way you would like. If you are honest with yourself, how does your body feel in that situation? What is your genuine emotional response to what is going on? Are you angry, sad, or scared about it? Notice how you feel. How many times have you felt this way in the past? Now, let yourself feel this emotion, and discover what specifically your emotion is about. Behind whatever your emotion points to is the issue that you are resisting and where you are in need of remembrance. Open to receiving support, and see how your experience of this situation changes.

Chapter Six

Issues with God

We start feeling that we are real and the Divine is an idea.
By the end, we discover it is really the other way around.

You might be saying, "Great! I understand so far. I need to feel my real emotions, face what is upsetting me in my life, discover what I am telling myself these problem means for me, and turn in remembrance to the Divine. But, what if I have issues with God?"

I have found that most issues with God take two forms. The first is that someone gave us a description of God that did not work for us. The second is that God has not come through and given us the life we wanted. In workshops, people constantly tell me, when they hear me say the word God, they are immediately reminded of some unsatisfactory experience from their past when someone told them who God was. This is usually a "fire-and-brimstone, born in sin, gonna get you kind of God. I will ask them why that felt so wrong. What inner sense of the Divine did that description go against? They will often describe a feeling of love, peace, mercy, compassion, and other feelings that are close to their hearts. This is the Divine from whom we seek guidance and support. We do not turn to the one that does not feel right. Instead, we turn to the one that our heart has always believed in. Rather than throwing the baby out with the bathwater, we open to the highest and most beautiful light we can conceive of and put our faith in that.

The other type of issues with God comes as a result of the events of our lives. God doesn't show up as a long-bearded gentleman doing this and that to us. We blame the Divine because God could have made it so the things that hurt us wouldn't have happened. This is another way to keep ourselves out of our experience. If we are in the conversation of whether or not a situation was fair, we do not have to face the things that are painful to us. We have decided the Divine plan is no good without seeing it through to the end. We never realize the ease that follows difficulty and, ultimately, the sense of being complete in both.

We also get upset with God when we turn to the Divine in times of need and it doesn't work. This usually means God did not change the situation into what we wanted it to be. Often when we are faced with adversity in our lives, we first try to deal with it on our own. Secondly, we look to someone or something to make it better. Thirdly, we turn to God, asking the Divine for what we want. If we do this without acknowledging our need for guidance, we are acting as if God is our hired hand. We say, "I have decided that what is happening should not be happening. I am calling You in to either make it right or show me how I can. If you don't come through and make things how I have decided they should be, then I my faith is shaken." Most of the time, when we are not getting anything from the practice of remembrance, it is because we are asking for guidance regarding our problems instead of support for our issues. We have not yet turned with compassion to the parts of ourselves that believe we must live in a way that doesn't feel good and acknowledge our need for support.

I have heard people say, "Where was God when I was going through such and such?" If we can ask that question, we must have made it through. The real question is, "Do we stay present and open to the support of God? Or, do we follow our reactions when painful things happen? If you remember, I said there are two fundamental beliefs required for spiritual healing. First, Divine support is available in every situation. Second, because we don't know what we are growing into, we do not know what experiences we need go through in order to become it. When we turn to God to get us out of our problems, we turn our connection into a strategy of resistance. It is easy to take issue with God, but it is not always so easy to face what we do not like in life and acknowledge that what we believe about these events needs guidance and support.

The Divine has already given us everything we need to handle what happens in life when the spirit was breathed into us. Until we have a direct experience of that spirit, we believe things have to go a certain way. The truth is that we contain all of the resources we will ever need when we give our connection a real chance.

All of us have misconceptions about God. As long as we have conceptions about God, they are going to be misconceptions. Through our connection, we grow in our experience of God in a moment-by-moment living way. This washes away our need to define the Divine. As we practice remembrance, the incredible beauty of God humbles us more and more and leaves us in awe at the magnitude of God's display. Gratitude replaces our issues with God and we fall in love with the Divine as we participate in the endless revelation.

Chapter Summary

1. People usually have issues with the Divine for three reasons:
    a. They received an unsatisfactory definition for the Divine that went against their own inner knowing.
    b. The Divine allowed something to happen to them that they did not want to happen.
    c. The Divine did not come through for them and change what they asked Him to change
2. The Divine you are asked to turn to is the one who feels the most right to your heart.
3. Questioning whether or not something that happened is right or fair is a form of resistance that keeps us from getting the insight we need.
4. Only when we are willing to go all the way through a difficult situation with the Divine will we discover spiritual sufficiency.

Exercise

If you have issues with God, ask yourself what you are upset about. What happened to cause you to feel this way about the Divine? Identify what upset you about this situation. What have you been telling yourself that it means for you? Is what you are telling yourself about this situation feel like the voice of the highest and most beautiful light? If not, then what does that light have to say? Go beyond your ideas of God, and open to receiving love and support in this place. Notice what happens.

Chapter Seven

The Healing Process

The first thing the fish must say is, I think there is
something wrong with this camel ride...
—Rumi

To summarize what we have talked about so far, we start with the statement that difficult situations happen to everyone. A difficult situation is one that upsets us and in which we then feel some version of angry, sad, or scared about what is going on. These emotions specifically point to the events or circumstances that are upsetting us and identify our problems. Problems are the catalysts for our issues that are at the root of what is upsetting us. Issues are our experiences of these circumstances and what we tell ourselves these problems mean for us. They reveal the places we are not yet aware of our sufficiency in the Divine. Here, we reach the crossroads of remembrance and resistance. If what we believe about a situation is unsupportive, remembrance tells us that we are in need of Divine Support. We are essentially remembering that we are always sufficed and reaching out to the Divine presence for guidance. When in resistance, we forget about our connection to the Divine and believe the situation must change before we will be whole again. We then come up with or search for reasons that explain what is causing us to be in this situation. To do this, we create stories. Stories are our explanations of why we have problems and what must we must do before we will be sufficed again. They lock us into our suffering by explaining what is responsible for the pain of our issues. Resistance tries to get us out of our problems by focusing on the stories of the lower self that explain why we are in difficult circumstances. Not only does this keep us from moving through what hurts, it makes the situation worse with actions based in upset emotions. Spiritual healing is the process of disengaging from our stories, facing our problems, acknowledging our issues, and opening to the Divine for support and guidance to discover our sufficiency in God.

A Common Thread

This process applies to every type of unsatisfactory experience. I have worked with people who were chronically sick, in troubled relationships, or were trying to get their company back on track. In each situation, all of them had one thing in common. Something was happening in their life that was upsetting them, and they could not find resolution. Regardless of whether the problem showed up as a physical disease, emotional distress, relationship difficulties, or job and career issues, the process looked the same in each case.

Spiritual healing is a process of self-love. It starts by becoming aware that something is troubling us and caring enough about ourselves to address it. One thing I hope you take away from this book is that, when something bothers you, hurts, or doesn't feel right, you stop and take notice. Don't ignore it, tough it out, work around it, act like it doesn't matter, or try to explain it away. This is our heart's way of telling us that we need guidance.

Not everything that happens causes us distress. While we can sometimes handle seemingly terrible situations with grace, the simplest things can drive us crazy other times. Each of us has to admit to ourselves when the events of life affect us. Many times, people deny the fact that they are troubled and spend a lot of time acting like everything is OK. You hear people say that things are going bad, but they are trying to not let it get to them. Unfortunately, it already has gotten to them. It is a part of their lives. It takes greater courage to admit that there is something bothering us than it does to act like nothing is wrong.

I had a client who came to see me. His life seemed to be falling apart on every level. He said he was incredibly over-whelmed and did not know how to do it anymore. I asked, "Do what?" He answered, "Hold it together." I asked if he knew how to be overwhelmed, and he said, "Oh yeah, everything in my being is overwhelmed." When I asked what he was overwhelmed about, he said that nothing was working out. As he faced this problem, he became aware that he was telling himself that he was doomed to struggle. When he acknowledged this issue and began the remembrance, his spirit opened like the sail on a ship. He realized this was a picture from his past and he had never walked through his disappointment before. As he experienced a deeper quality of sustenance, his being relaxed and what he needed to do became evident. His thoughts, words, and actions were based in this new quality, and his problems were soon resolved

The Healing Process

Before we start any healing work on our selves, we always start with a prayer. The prayers we say are not for God. They are for our selves because we are the ones who need the benefit of praying. In our prayer we are opening ourselves to Highest, most beautiful reality we can conceive of to receive healing and guidance. We are humbly admitting that we need help and are reminding our selves that, at the core of our problem, is our need for Divine support. We are remembering the Divine is the source that suffices us and all healing comes from that source. We are affirming that God is the healer and we need Divine guidance to come into peace with the events of our lives. This type of prayer orients us in the direction of the Divine and creates a vessel in which healing can happen.

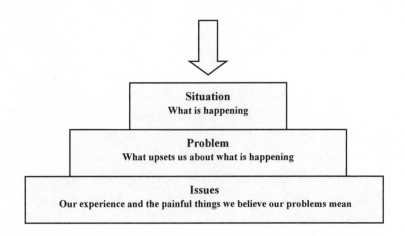

Next, we think about the situation we are struggling with. We take some time and go over what is happening in our lives.

Whatever is happening represents the physical manifestation of our troubles or the leaves on the tree. We now have to work our way back down the pyramid to the root of our issues.

There is a difference between what is happening and what bothers us about it.

We ask ourselves, "What about this situation is most upsetting? What are we angry, frustrated, sad, scared, or overwhelmed about?" There is great freedom in just speaking what is really upsetting us. People will talk all around it but not come out and say what is really bothering them. We must be honest with ourselves, even if we are embarrassed or ashamed to admit what we are upset about. Once we know what we are upset about, we will have identified our problem.

Most of the time, when I am working with people, I discover they have remained stuck because they have not faced what is really upsetting them and have been working on their story instead. It is easy to become caught up in trying to fix the reasons we are upset rather than facing what we are upset about. When identifying our problem, we only want to know what we are upset about. We don't want to explain why we are not at peace, what might make us feel better, or theorize what might have led up to this moment. We simply want to identify what is bothering us.

Once we are facing our problem, the next step is to become aware of what it feels like to be in this situation and what we are telling our selves this problem means for us. We are searching for the painful conclusion this problem has led us to make the issue beneath our problem. We know we have discovered our issue when our heart feels burdened as if we are stuck with something less than fulfilling.

When we release our resistance and own our emotions, we are left with what is uncomfortable, that is, our issues. We are allowing ourselves to feel what we may have been running from and denying for a long time. Everything inside us may hate feeling this way. It might seem like the last place we would want to go. This may be precisely the reason we have stayed stuck. The way out is through the pain of our issues. It is usually the one door we have not tried.

God says, give the good news to my people
that when I am called, I respond.

We can now acknowledge the pain of our issues. Remember, there is no space inside of us to receive Divine insight until we admit that what we are believing about a situation needs support. We turn in compassion to these parts of our selves and place them in the Hands of the Highest most Beautiful Reality for support and guidance. Healing happens when the insights from the Divine replace the issues of our self. We continue remembering our name for the Most High, receiving and listening to what comes to us, until we are at peace.

I was teaching a few years ago. Sharing these same state-ments, a man said, "This is my story." He was diagnosed with throat cancer and went to every doctor. He had every treatment available, but nothing was slowing the cancer. Finally, he was on his deathbed and said to God, "If you want me to die, I will die. If you want me to live, I will live. I am in pain, and I surrender my life to you." His problem was that he was dying, but the issue being brought up by the cancer was one of living a life that meant nothing. In that moment, he cried out to God and let go of trying to make it better, felt the pain of his issue, and let go into God's care. His heart began to fill with love, and he felt himself being carried in a way he had never experienced. Years of pain were being washed away as he faced what he had been running from his whole life. He experienced picture after picture of painful situations in his life release while receiving insight and care from God. His spirit soared. Every ounce of his being was able to say yes to life, even with all of its difficulties, because he realized he had a connection to a force inside of him that sufficed him in every situation. He drank in the love and support of God and allowed the places inside him that had been empty for so long to be filled. By letting go into the pain of possibly dying and all that cancer meant, he discovered a resource inside he had never dreamed. Yet, he realized he had been missing it his whole life. Not long after this experience, he went into remission and is now cancer-free.

Clearing Away the Layers of Issues

After we receive from the Divine, something still might be troubling us. We may feel better because we received guidance, but we are not totally at peace. It is important to notice what is bothering us about what we received from the Divine or what remains unresolved. These are called the "yeah buts." We must acknowledge our "yeah buts" and not ignore them because there is now something else that is upsetting us. In these instances we need to go through the process again. If we are willing to face what bothers us about what the Divine has showed us or what remains unresolved, we will uncover the next layer of our issues. Memories in the form of pictures might surface, and we may feel as if we are two, five, or twelve years old again. We may discover beliefs about how we believed we needed to live our lives. Certain kinds of circumstances in which we are not sure how to apply what we received from the Divine may come to mind. Or we may simply feel the pain of living without knowing we were supported for so long.

As we work, many layers of our original issue often surface to be healed. We must also acknowledge and care for them by opening them to divine support. In this way, we uncover the pictures and issues from our past that are still affecting us today. As we work through the first one, we uncover the next and the next until we are completely at peace with what comes to us from the Divine. We may sometimes need to turn in remembrance with several issues before we reach a sense of harmony. The issues from our past percolate to the surface when the necessary love and support to heal and guide them are available. It is like picking up a string and following it where it leads, staying in remembrance until we feel at peace inside. People will often stop with not hurting. Instead, we keep going until we feel whole again. We stay in remembrance until every part of us that believed we had to live in an unfulfilling way has been released. We know we are through what was troubling us when we experience a sense of well-being, things start to make sense, and we feel the relief associated with releasing what was causing us pain.

I had a client who was suffering from chronic headaches that had developed into a seizure disorder. When she faced what upset her about this, she became aware that her experience was one of being squeezed. She believed she could not go on. As she acknowledged this issue in remembrance, she discovered that the Divine was supporting her in this experience. She felt better, but she began to worry about all of the obligations of her life. When she faced all of these obligations, they felt like a mountain weighing down on her. She realized her seizures were the manifestation of her struggles under the weight of these burdens. When she acknowledged this next layer of her issues, she discovered that the Divine was giving her what she needed to handle each of these situations one at a time. The feeling of being burdened was replaced by one of confident capability. Her headaches and seizures ceased plaguing her as she handled each of these situations.

In spiritual healing, we have the advantage of knowing where we are headed because all paths lead to sufficiency in God. How we are going to get there and what it will look like waits to be seen. It is necessary to be patient with ourselves and take as much time with Divine support and guidance as we need. We do not know what is going to come up once we turn to the Divine, but healing happens when we give ourselves the space to feel what we need to feel while receiving guidance and support. Many people who start out wanting to heal an illness or broken relationship discover their entire lives change through this process. Attitudes, beliefs, and old wounds are washed away. When we finally get through what was troubling us, we often get much more than the healing of our original problem. God gives us more than we knew to ask for when He moves us into a life of harmony and beauty. The issue that started as an obstacle to our happiness becomes the means of realizing a truly fulfilling life.

The balance is in being expectant of God's generosity and patient with the Divine decree. When we reach out God, we are open to being healed and guided in one moment. This is expectancy. We have the patience, however, to go through and acknowledge whatever feelings, memories, and experiences come up for us on this healing journey. Many people turn to God and do not expect very much. When we turn to God in this way, there is no place for the love to come in. It is like complaining that no one is calling while we keep the phone off the hook. In order to receive healing and guidance, we must open our hearts to the Most High, whose support and guidance is greater than and beyond any trial. It only takes is a crack in the door.

Surrendering

The real wisdom of why we are going through a particular situation comes on the other side of experience. It would be nice if all of us had the answers before facing a difficult situation, but the truth is that we do not, not consciously anyway. That is where the Divine comes in. This Highest Light carries us past where we have gone before and unearths our spirit from the lower nature. First, however, we must go through the experience in order to clean or clear away the stories, pictures, and attachments of the lower nature that are covering the innate knowing and power of the spirit.

First the feeling and then the healing,
not the other way around.

We do not know what changes we are being asked to go through until after we have surrendered to the events of our lives and followed the guidance of the Divine. The opposite of resistance is surrender. We are surrendering to the fact that we are human beings who get upset, don't have all of the answers, and are not in control of everything that happens in our lives. God is the one who knows what we need to grow and what we need to release in the process of growing. Our sufficiency in the Divine is the only constant in the ups and downs of our lives. There is nothing to hold onto except this connection. The answers are not going to come from our self. Rather, we are letting go to discover who we will be on the other side of what pains us, allowing God to both guide and care for us. Many people believe, in order to be surrendered, they have to be in calm acceptance of what is happening. It can sometimes be just the opposite. Being in surrender to our lives means we are willing to experience them as is.

You can sometimes know too much for your own good. When I was teaching a workshop, I once had a bad flu virus. I was staying on the eleventh floor of the hotel. The workshop I was leading was on the second floor. I had spent an hour in my hotel room trying to surrender so I could feel better. I was saying to God, "Okay, I accept I am sick. I am in your hands. Do with me as you will." Nothing was changing, and I was being as accepting as I could be. When I got in the elevator, I was feeling so bad that I was dizzy. I finally surren-

dered into actually feeling sick and realized I was telling myself that this meant I was all alone and forgotten in my suffering. As I acknowledged this experience and began the remembrance, I immediately felt God's response and support. Miraculously, my fever broke before I hit the second floor. I was then able to teach the rest of the workshop.

Real Security

It's on the other side of surrender that we discover that all the things we were holding onto and drawing our safety from were really keeping us from being free. Our spirit, or who we really are, is from God and was never really in jeopardy from the events of life. That's real security. Under all of our stories are the unresolved emotions. Under all of the unresolved emotions are the problems we are upset about. Under these problems are the issues we need to walk though in order to grow in our experience of sufficiency and purify ourselves of our lower natures.

Healing does not always look the way we would like. It does not always mean that we get better or the relationship mends. Being healed means we can move forward in our lives from a place of peace, feeling guided and cared for. Most times, this leads to the healing of our original problem. Other times, we receive what we need to move on in harmony. Surrendering to the events of life and moving in harmony with God ensures that, whatever happens, we will be fully alive and moving through it with love. We will be reborn into the present moment with a greater realization of the Divine and our own spiritual nature. As long as we believe the experiences that tell us we can only be happy in certain situations, we will never know the real joy that comes from simply being.

The art of surrendering is certainly a lost one in our culture. Students ask me to tell them what it would be like to let go of control and allow the flow of life to take them. They often fear that, if they let go, the things that are important to them won't be handled. I tell them to imagine their life without their neurosis, and they would have it. If you let go of worry, managing things, reactions, and control, what would you have? Stop and feel that for a moment. Spiritual healing is a death of sorts. What survives this death is everything that is real and good.

The Divine loves and knows us more intimately than we know ourselves. In spiritual healing, we only have to be open to being beautified. Pain is not in this world to punish us. It is here so we can discover a life beyond the comings and goings of things. When gold has been in the fire, its true beauty can be seen. God never takes anything from who we think we are without giving us something better in return. That something better is the experience and knowledge of our sufficiency in the Divine. Everything else passes and goes away. Why live our lives for what is fleeting? After a while, this process of dying/beautification becomes a way of life without end. So many people on spiritual paths are trying to determine who they really are or achieve some state of being. A more accurate journey would be to let go of who we are not in order to make room for the All that is.

Getting in Rhythm

As we practice and apply the healing process over time, we become more adept at moving through the steps. It is a lot like when we are first learning to dance. In the beginning, we need to think about where to place our feet, how to hold our hands, and head, all while keeping track of both the music and our partner. Soon, however, these movements become second nature, and we are just dancing. When awareness of our experience and remembrance become a way of life, we can move through the process very quickly, without having to think about the steps.

Each time that I am struggling in my life, I find I am unaligned with some part of the healing process. Each stage represents a valuable life lesson. The opening prayer represents living a life with the awareness that we are in God's hands. Owning our emotions and admitting when we are upset strengthens personal honesty and integrity. Recognizing when something is troubling us and identifying it develops self-awareness. Facing what upsets us develops courage, and acknowledging our issues fosters self-love and mercy. Being willing to admit we need guidance engenders humility and teaches us to receive support. Trading the guidance of our self for the guidance of the Divine helps us realize spiritual sufficiency. Finally, going through a painful situation with the support of God allow us to show up for all that life has to offer and experience a sense of happiness and well-being that is beyond the comings and goings of things and events.

Chapter Summary: The Healing Process

1. Start with a prayer. Ask that God bless this healing and help you receive whatever will bring you into harmony with the Divine. Affirm God is the One who is the healer and the One who knows what you need.

2. Identify what is troubling you.

3. Notice how you feel about what is happening. Are you angry, sad, or scared? Own your emotions.

4. What are you upset about? What exactly are your emotions pointing to?

5. Become aware of your experience of this problem. What do you believe this situation means for you? Acknowledge your issue in compassion, and turn in remembrance to God.

6. Stay in remembrance, allowing the experiences that surface to be cared for and washed by God until you receive what you need to be at peace.

7. Return to the original situation that was troubling you. Notice what has changed. If there is still something that is bothering you, return to the second step.

8. When you feel at peace. Spend some time in gratitude for what you received in remembrance.

Exercise

Apply the seven steps from above to something you are currently struggling with. What changes do you notice? If you find yourself becoming stuck anywhere in the process, go back to the step before the one you had trouble with. Start again from there.

Chapter Eight

The Beautification of the Self

Oh God, I seek justice from this justice seeking self.
—Rumi

Each time we move through a painful event with the
support of the Divine, our faith deepens. Along with our faith,
something else—our character—grows. Character boils down
to what we do with what we are given or how we respond to the
cards we are dealt. Our actions demonstrate how we feel inside.
Those feelings are based in whether or not we are aware of our
sufficiency in the Divine. The more aware we are of Divine care,
the easier it is to respond in a way that is beautiful and create
balance in all of our relationships. A friend of mine will often
say that, if you want to be generous, than it is good to be rich.
In this case, he means rich in spirit. This sense of abundant
richness and clarity will remain elusive as long as we believe our
well-being is dependent on things and situations instead of
the spirit. Whether in relationship with ourselves, another
person, or the various responsibilities of our lives, the beauty
and solidity of our character is evident when sourced in Divine
sufficiency.

Spiritual Maturity

In order for the self to be in harmony, the spirit must have ascendancy over the lower nature. When the self is free from the veils of the lower nature, the spirit informs the mind and the emotions as to what is needed in the ever-changing moment. If the lower nature resists an experience, our spiritual connection becomes eclipsed. Then the self does not receive the clear information it needs to act in harmony. Because our bodies move at the will of our minds and emotions, without the right information, we are soon doing and saying things that make our lives more difficult.

There is more to becoming adult than reaching maturity. The self also must mature. I don't think it is any secret that we have two- and three-year-old selves running around in adult bodies. To become truly adult, we must free the spirit from the attachments of the lower nature so the self can display the full splendor of the breath of God. Each of us is born with a lower nature. The journey of becoming fully human is the process of freeing our spirits from the influence of it while being in the body. Each of us are journeying to, "Be in the world, but not of the world."

In life, we have the events that happen to us, but, more importantly, we have what these events mean to us and the feelings they generate. The events of our lives are like a mirror that reflects the state of our heart back to us. Our reactions to these events reveal the extent of our certainty in Divine care to us. It is easy to forget that these reflections are passing and it is the realizations of our heart we take with us. It is of no use to get all of the things of our lives together just in time to die and leave them behind. Using the events of our lives as the crucible in which we develop our character is the work that will bear fruit in this life and the next.

Purifying the Self

In any given moment, either the spirit or the body is most prominently guiding the self. This relationship determines the relative refinement or coarseness of our individual selves (character). The struggle for authority over the self between body and spirit, that is, higher and lower nature, characterizes the human experience. The self contains both body and spirit, so we cannot claim to be totally one or the other. We can be both incredibly divine and incredibly petty in the space of several moments. The difficulty of being human is in balancing both aspects. As spirit gains ascendancy over the body, the self beautifies and acts in harmony with the Divine more frequently through the ups and downs of life. The times of greatest potential for refinement are when things do not go our way. These situations are referred to as being in the fire. They place us at the crossroad of resistance and remembrance and asks which road we will choose. The question in these moments is, "Do we follow our emotional reactions and resist the situation? Or, do we acknowledge our issues and need for the guidance and support of God?"

Our selves, with their combination of body and spirit, are like gold that has not been purified. They need to be put in the fire in order to separate pure from impure. The impurities we are being cleansed of are not the desires of the lower nature. Rather, they are the reliance our self has on them for guidance. Many people spend so much energy trying to change the opinions of the lower nature. They feel embarrassed about their thoughts and feelings, and they are ashamed of the ways they get upset in their lives. Our lower nature will always be the lower nature and will consistently believe that things not going our way means suffering. We get into trouble when we let the lower nature inform our lives. We are not trying to change the lower nature. We are simply trying to purify our selves from the influence it has over us by busying ourselves with the guidance of the Divine. Our lower nature feeds on attention. The more time we spend listening to its opinions or trying to address its concerns, the stronger it becomes. When we acknowledge that our self's version of events is deficient and needs support, our attention shifts to the Divine. Each time we acknowledge our need for Divine support, the voice of the lower self weakens, and the gold of our selves becomes more pure. Experiencing the superiority of Divine guidance and the beauty we create in our lives by listening to this source causes the lower nature to lose some of its credibility with the self. Over time, the guidance of the Divine becomes increasingly pronounced until it consumes our attention.

Difficult situations cannot weaken the self's hold on us. They only help us to realize that what we are listening to is not leading us in a direction we want to go. We weaken the hold our lower nature has over us by trading our issues for the insights of the Divine. This can only be done when we honestly see the greater beauty of the Divine insight for ourselves. Then we willingly and gratefully make the trade. In this way, we surrender ourselves to the Divine through love with our eyes wide open. It isn't because we are being forced to and will be punished if we don't. Spiritual traditions teaches us that, when God wants to give us something, He makes us aware of our need for it so we will make the decision to ask for help. Walking with God is a process of beautification. It isn't one of shame and coercion. Over time, as we make trade after trade, we become certain that our lives are better lived as a reflection of God's qualities than a display of our own.

Each time we go through the healing process, a pathway is worn in our consciousness. When we start on this journey, the path of resistance is a fairly worn road while the path of the spirit is literally the road less traveled. Whenever we turn to God, we are weaning ourselves from the input of the lower self. Over time, the path of spirit becomes increasingly pronounced, and the road of resistance falls into obscurity and disrepair. Finally turning to God becomes second nature. This is achieved in two ways. By applying the practice of acknowledgement/remembrance over time and the magnetic attraction that happens between God and us. We are soon overcome by the beauty of the Divine and realize there is no better place to be.

Moving in Harmony

The gold of our spirits is in no jeopardy from the fires of purification. What truly gives us life, power, knowledge, love, and form is far from being in danger from the events of life. When the gold of our selves becomes purified, it not only becomes cleaner and more beautiful. It also becomes malleable. This malleability allows it to be molded into whatever shape the moment demands. We are then able to be in right relationship with the various aspects of our lives and give each thing what it needs. Every movement and form then displays another facet of our relationship with the Divine.

We are constantly being passed back and forth between the two hands of the Divine. One hand is called ease, and the other is called difficulty. In spiritual healing, we remind our selves that both of these hands are the Hands of the Most Merciful. God sometimes gives us ease and frees us from our attachments. Other times we are given difficulty and shown the limit of those attachments. To be in harmony with ease, we must be willing to release our attachments and expand. To be in harmony with difficulty, we must be willing to feel the pain of having attachments and our need to be free of them. When God comes to us as ease , harmony is to be found in expanding. When he comes as difficulty, harmony is found in being low. As we disconnect from the opinions our self has about these risings and fallings and attach ourselves to the Divine, we discover that both of these faces are the Face of Divine care that leads us into greater realization. The key is not losing hope in His help when we are being brought low and not feeling we are permanently free of difficulty because we are being raised up.

The opinions and objections the self has of these movements are the impurities that keep us from being able to move into whatever form the moment demands. As we increasingly rely on our spiritual connection to guide us through these moments, we discover sufficiency in both easy and hard times. We stop labeling experiences as good or bad and continually discover that we are complete with God in both.

A simple test of our orientation is the "oh crap" test. When something happens that is not what you planned, do you exclaim "Oh crap!" or "Oh God!" "Oh crap" means "Here is another situation I am going to have to deal with that has bad implications for me." "Oh God" is said with the knowledge that the Divine is available to guide us through what is happening. This simple test will show you which path is your knee-jerk reaction. "Oh crap" leads us to the management of the self. "Oh God" leads us to security in our connection. As our practice develops, we spend less time with the self in "Oh crap" and more time receiving from the Divine.

The Stages of Development

Although we continually fluctuate from moment to moment, the process of refining the self basically goes through three stages:

Stage One: Objecting

In this stage, the lower nature and its emotional reactions rule the self. This means we act on the conclusions of our issues, backed up with the explanations of our stories that tell us why things have to be this way, and do things that are not balanced or beneficial. If we are angry, we fight. If we are scared, we run. If we are sad, we despair. A person in this stage is often irrational, not in control of their reactions, and seems at the affect of life. For example, a friend may say something that hurts our feelings. We then get angry. We follow our issues and stories, telling us to close our heart to our friend (issue) because he or she does not care about us. (story). Because our stories identify our friend's unkindness as the reason we need to close our heart, we do and say angry things directed at our friend's unkindness, which creates more problems between the two of us.

Acting out of hurt and reaction, we get more of what hurt and made us react in the first place, that is, a damaged relationship. To move on to the second stage, we must notice that we are emotional and acting from pain. We then must stop and realize we need support. We no longer return to this stage when we have finally learned not to take action when we are upset.

Stage Two: Acknowledgment

The self realizes that following its emotional reactions doesn't lead to resolution. In this stage, we do not act on our emotions and begin to look inside. Although we want to act in an upset way, we resist these urges. Because we have stopped resisting what upsets us, we are left with our experience. In this stage we need to stop trying to manage our experience or figure out how to make it better. Instead, we open to Divine support. It is important that we are careful not to become caught in our stories and believe they are the reasons we are having a difficult time.

This can be an awkward stage because we are in between guidance and struggle. We may not be in harmony yet, but we know that what we are doing is not it. It requires a willingness to be vulnerable, to drop our desire to be right, and feel our need for guidance. We are both helping our self by reminding it of the nearness of Divine support and opposing our self by reigning in our emotional reactions and stories. For example, a friend may say something that hurts our feelings. We get angry, but, before we respond, we notice we are upset and stop. Now, instead of focusing on what we believe is causing us to be upset we look inside to our selves, acknowledge our issues and seek a way of balance through Divine guidance. If, we stay inside in remembrance, we will be able to move onto the third stage.

Stage Three: Faith and Trust

The self acknowledges the pain of its issues and places them in the hands of the Divine. The person allows himself or herself to be supported by the Divine, no longer defends against certain kinds of experience, and does whatever is in harmony with the moment. For example, a person may hurt our feelings, and we become angry. Not only do we not allow the anger to run us into harmful actions, we acknowledge the painful issues we draw from that experience and turn to God for support and guidance. We continue to repeat the name of the Divine, listening with our entire beings until we receive what returns us to a state of peace. From this place in our example, we might realize that what the person said has nothing to do with us and our friend really needs more support, not less. The action that comes from Divine insight is the real medicine for this situation. What appeared to initially hurt our friendship may turn out to strengthen it in the end. This third stage has no end because there is no end to our movement in the Divine. Only when a person has no attachment to the kinds of experience they are given is their room for the full majesty and beauty of the Divine qualities contained in the spirit to be realized.

In the first stage, our actions and responses are still part of the problem. In the second, we have disengaged from being part of the problem but do not yet embody the solution. In the third stage, the support of the Divine has lifted us out of the problem and guided us into becoming the solution.

A simplified way of looking at these three stages is to ask ourselves, "What do we do in the face of difficult circumstances?" Do we become upset and take emotional actions? Do we stop ourselves from taking emotional actions but try and manage our experience or figure out how to make things go the way we would like? Or, do we acknowledge our need for guidance and support and listen until we are at peace and can respond with clarity? Our answer to this question will indicate the relative refinement of our selves and our ability to be in harmony with the changes of life.

Moving through these stages and beautifying our character mirrors the healing process. In the first stage, we learn to recognize when we are upset by the events of our lives, stop ourselves from taking further action, and realize we need support before moving forward. In the second stage, we leave behind the explanations for our unhappiness and acknowledge that we need Divine Guidance if we hurt. In the third step, we learn to receive and surrender to that guidance in order to put forth beautiful responses into our lives. In each stage, the common denominator is turning from the self to the Divine. First, we turn from our reactions. Then we turn from the efforts and management of our selves. Finally, in order to become a new creation, we turn from our selves and who we thought we were.

Uncovering the Spirit

There is no end to the journey of being created anew because there is no end to the Divine qualities inherent in our spirits. Therefore, we are never done evolving and growing in our experience of the Divine. What grows and beautifies is our character and how we respond to the ever-changing moments of our lives.

The relationship between body and spirit is like a light inside a glass lamp. The glass represents the body or lower nature; the light represents the spirit or higher nature. Depending on how clear the glass is, the light from the outside will appear more or less brilliant. Weaning the self from the reactions of the lower nature is like cleaning the glass. The cleaner it becomes, the more beautiful and brilliant the light appears. The light, like our spirit, is infinitely pure, but, based on the purity of the glass, that purity shows through differently into the experience of our selves. We continue being purified in the third stage until we move in harmony with spirit. At this point, the spirit's purity manifests without being altered by the attachments of the lower nature. The glass is so clean that there only appears to be light. At this point, regardless of what the world does, we respond from alignment with spirit.

I like to say that all self-definitions have a shelf life of one moment. If they last longer than that, who we believe we are gets in the way of the unending unfolding of our spirits. One of the first things my teacher told me was to be the son or daughter of my moment. This means allowing the moment to give birth to us in the form that fits it. We have been trained to believe that life should be easy and beautiful. If it is difficult, we believe this means we must not be doing something right. We then avoid the painful situations that are the catalyst for our growth. Our lower natures want what they want so they can stay in control, believing this guarantees we will get what we need. When we live this way, we forget the self's need to grow in its experience of the Divine.

Mystics often refer to the spirit as a buried treasure. The difficulty of life causes us to dig deep enough to find it. The spirit reaches out to God, like a seed beneath the soil that has an innate knowing of the sun and a faith in the one who created it to be a tree. In this reaching out, the spirit is uncovered. As we uncover this treasure, we also get rid of all of the dirt that was keeping us from knowing our potential. Like a tree, our spirit is rooted in the earth of our body, but the fruit is to be found above ground after receiving the light of the Divine sun.

True Perfection

Until we are willing to allow ourselves to feel the pain of a given situation, our spirit cannot reach out to God for the right medicine. As people, we often greatly underestimate the power of our own spiritual connection to carry us through what hurts. The things we attach to become who we believe we are. We then forget the beauty of dying to who we have been and the wonder of being created new. As I said earlier, the qualities of the Divine are reflected inside of us in the form of our spirit. However, there is a vast difference between having these qualities and realizing them. When we open to the light of the Divine through our spirits, the qualities of the self become increasingly refined. This refinement is a transparency that allows the beauty of the Divine qualities to shine through into our lives.

Staying in the flow of life is about being fluid. If we identify with and get attached to things being a certain way and being a certain someone in relationship to them. When the next moment brings us a situation that challenges that form, we are unable to move forward. The longer we stop there, the less we participate in the Divine moment. This cuts us off from benefiting from and experiencing the qualities that are inherent in our spirit. Now we cannot really cut our selves off from these qualities. We just limit your conscious participation. Our spirits all contain the ability to experience the Divine qualities. We only experience and participate in them to different degrees. Each one of us will taste death, but not everyone really lives. When we allow our preferences for life to cut us off from the Divine, it only does so in our experience, not in actuality. We live, but not really. We know, but not really. We love, but not really. All of this is because we don't participate. Our attachment to things being a certain way drains the life out of life. Is it any wonder our bodies, relationships, and jobs soon follow suit?

To stay fluid, we need to open to the Divine in every moment. Acknowledge our need for divine revelation and not to say now that I have realized this or experienced such and such I have arrived and know how this existence works. I call this the one realization fits all syndrome. It says, "If I can just do something right, get over this issue, fix some problem, or figure out some way of being, then I'll finally be free from struggling. This means I will finally get it. It is the answer of how to be so I won't be needy anymore."

This is where I started my spiritual path. I was trying to figure what I had to do or understand in order to free myself from pain and walk (or rather float) through life unfazed. Believe me, I was disappointed when I found out this was not the case. I actually had to show up in every moment of life, feel my real feelings, and allow myself to be molded by the Divine rather than how I wanted to feel or who I wanted to be. This required real surrender. I liked the feeling of having it all together, and I was not very happy with the parts of life that were not cooperating. To let this go was going to require real trust. As I worked the process, however, I discovered there wasn't a magic bullet and searching for it was actually keeping me from embracing the full spectrum of life. I began to discover that I often felt weak. I often did not know what to do. I often went into situations that were outside of my ability to control or make right, but none of that cut me off from the Divine sustenance that was available through my own spirit. I also realized the pain I was feeling in these situation was really the places in myself that did not know the full measure of God's care being stretched. These situations were forcing me to let go of who I thought I was and open to more.

By staying open to receiving God's love and support, I have found that I am sufficed through anything life has to deal me. The best part is that it isn't all up to me. In fact, my being OK has already been taken care of. Every day, I am increasingly realizing that the Divine has no interest in making me perfect in any way that I understand the word. Instead, the Divine is interested in keeping me in wonder and amazement at the limitless ways that life makes itself known. Only in the limitlessness of being created new in every moment can our beings taste true perfection, an experience without horizon.

> *God's perfection is so large that it makes room for the human's imperfections. The human's idea of perfection is so small that nothing at all fits in.*

A New Creation

Our willingness to surrender our idea of what our life means to us makes room in our awareness for Divine revelation. The fact that yesterday's strength, knowledge, and capability are today's weakness, ignorance, and inability keeps us in relationship with God's strength, knowledge, and ability without end. The Divine plan for who we are becoming is revealed moment by moment, not all at once. By staying open to and surrendered to the moment, we are renewed and expanded in our experience of the Divine qualities and experience a greater refinement and beauty of our selves. In each instant, we are created new in a way that we did not expect or did not even know to ask for. Real happiness is based on the blessings that surprise us and renew our sense of wonder at life and Divinity. If we always got what we wanted or expected, we would always be who we already are. The wonder and excitement go out of life and it's just not worth living. Not for any self with a spirit in it. Eventually our attention never leaves the Divine. If we are given ease in our lives we thank God as our provider and if we are given difficulty we turn to God as our healer. As we keep our face turned toward the Divine we see God's Hand in every moment and lose our limited selves in the witnessing.

The Union

In His infinite love and care, God made the instrument of His support for us our very own spirit. The qualities of life, strength, sight, knowledge, and ability are truly the Divine's qualities manifesting through us. So the strength we feel within our own beings is really Divine strength, we only experience weakness when we claim that strength for our own. We cut our selves off from the source of strength by identifying it with one kind of power and trying to fit it into every situation. Sometimes, the true strength of a tree is in its ability to bend. Those who believe that strength is always standing straight will be broken by the wind of life. These qualities are so immense, like the sea, that there is no way we could hold the all, so we must be open to how they are displayed in our beings in each moment. The beauty of this process is that, in each moment, these qualities take on the limitless shapes of satisfaction that our needs require. The Divine makes itself known in this way. Like water, the spirit of revelation takes the shape of the cup. Because we have a cupful, we cannot claim that what is in our cup is the entire ocean. The joy is in witnessing the myriad shapes our cups/need can take and the myriad ways the water of the spirit can fill them. We are the place or the stage on which the Divine qualities makes themselves known without end and never the same way twice. The fact we are created with body and spirit, need, and its fulfillment is a testament to the unity of Divinity.

Chapter Summary

1. Walking through the difficult issues of our lives deepens our knowledge of God, which sets the tone for our character.
2. Character boils down to what we do with what we are given.
3. When the spirit is freed from the attachments of the body, the self becomes more mature and more beautiful as the light of the spirit shows through into our lives.
4. The self goes through three stages of development: objection, acknowledgement, and faith and trust.
5. There is no end to the third stage because there is no end to the qualities of God that can manifest in our lives.
6. As we walk with God, we experience the limitless ways our lives are the stage on which the Divine qualities are displayed.

Exercise

Take some time to identity the area of your life that needs support. Ask yourself, "Am I objecting and reacting emotionally to what is happening? Am I trying to figure out how to make the situation go the way I would like? Or, am I acknowledging my need for divine support and reaching out in remembrance?" If you are not in remembrance, practice the tools you have learned so far.

Chapter Nine

Assisting Others in Healing

It is of no use walking anywhere to preach,
unless our walking is our preaching.
—St. Francis of Assisi

As we have seen in the last several chapters, spiritual healing is based on remembering our connection to the Divine and discovering our sufficiency in each moment. While self-healing is built on remembrance, helping others is a process of reminding. One of our students once boiled down all of our work into the statement, "They love you and love you and love you until you get it." A healer's job is to remind a person of the nearness and availability of Divine support until they have a direct experience of it for themselves. It is not the job of the healer to come up with the answers. Rather, it is to point to the source from which all answers come. We simply serve as a reminder that, when a person calls out to the Divine, the Divine responds.

We cannot remind someone of this connection unless we have some degree of certainty for ourselves. In spiritual healing, we say, "First receive, then give." When we have walked through difficult situations with the support and guidance of the Divine, our heart carries the truth of that experience. We cannot ask someone to go somewhere we have not been willing to go ourselves. Each time we discover the support of the Divine in the midst of painful situations, we become more certain of finding that support in every moment. When helping another person, we are then able to listen to what is paining them and share in that experience without having to make it better or judging it as wrong. We can say to a person, "I hear, recognize, and feel that what you are going through is painful, and you feel as if you are unsupported and must live in a way that is unfulfilling. None of these feelings, however, cut you off from the Divine. Take some time to care for that experience by acknowledging it and opening it to the love and support of the Divine that responds when you call." In this way, we are standing with them in the places they need to acknowledge and feel. As we share in their experience, while maintaining certainty of Divine support, we become a bridge between them and the Divine. The more we are able to share in their experiences and the stronger our certainty of God's support becomes, the more trust and safety we will engender. This enables them to move quickly into their issues and go deeper in remembrance.

The Power of Faith

People often ask, "If God is the healer, why are some people better able to facilitate that healing than others?" The answer is faith. A measure of a healer is the measure of their faith in the Divine. Some people trust God only so far. As long as certain things happen and others don't, they trust. This creates a conditional faith. They are then able to hold people through certain experiences, but not in others. People with conditional faith may become caught in trying to fix the person or colluding with the idea that they don't have what they need. Healers who have surrendered all of their affairs to God and trust in Divine sufficiency, regardless of what comes, have a greater power of faith. They are able to transmit the reality of God's nearness, no matter what is happening in a person's life. This makes it easier for the person they are supporting to let go into what is troubling him or her and taste that support for him or herself.

> *I was once teaching in Texas. One of the participants thanked me for bringing through some much love and support in the weekend. I responded by saying that the love and support was there long before I arrived. I was simply guided stand in the truth of that Presence, regardless of what people shared to the contrary, until we were all certain of its presence.*

Certainty in Divine support cannot be bought or taught. It must be earned. We can say all of the right things, but, if our heart is not truly witnessing the hands of the Divine around our client, the transmission of safety will not be conveyed. This certainty comes as a gift from the Divine because of what God revealed to us about this support when we were going through similar situations.

There is a difference between being upset about what is happening in people's lives and acknowledging that what is happening is painful for them. In the latter example, we do not lose connection to Divine support. This gives them hope in the midst of their pain. When we become upset about what is happening, we can easily move into trying to fix their problems as if they are not suffced. Internally staying in remembrance for ourselves, when we are working with people, is necessary to hold all that they have to share. As they tell us about their struggles, we listen to what they say through the filter of remembrance. It is a lot like a serve and volley in tennis. They tell us what they are struggling with. Before we respond, we repeat our name for the Divine, examining what they have shared through this lens. In this way, we are trading our perceptions for our best approximation of the Divine's.

As healers, we walk the fine line between acknowledging people's pain and being certain of their sufficiency in God. An experience is painful until God reveals to them that the painful events in their lives don't mean what they believed they meant. Until that moment, it genuinely hurts, and we cannot discount or make light of their issues. Only when they see something from the Divine that changes their experience is spiritual sufficiency really true for them. Until that moment, we must be willing to acknowledge their pain while pointing them in the direction of the Divine until that inspiration happens. We know God suffices them in each moment, but the how of that is something that is shared between them and the Divine. The answer does not come from us. We, however, are willing to compassionately hang in there with whatever they are feeling or telling themselves until that communication happens. In this way, we are like earth for the person, giving them whatever they need to flower in their Divine connection.

Restoring Hope

The greatest thing you can give people going through painful situations is hope. The greatest hope is to be found in the Divine. This hope allows them to face what is painful and open to receiving Divine care. People resist painful situations because they do not believe there is a way for them to go through it and have what they need. A healer's heart says otherwise. It is this certainty and unconditional support that helps them face what is troubling them.

As the people we are supporting describe their situations, we are listening for what is specifically bothering them about what is going on. We are asking ourselves, "What are they actually upset about?" Until they face what is upsetting them, we cannot help them uncover the issues that need Divine support.

It is not always easy to stand with people as they face what is upsetting them. What they are facing may bring up places inside of us where we are uncertain of Divine support. In these moments, we must acknowledge what we are telling ourselves about what people are going through that is causing us to lose heart. We then can turn in remembrance and receive what returns us to certainty in the moment. Unless we go through this process for ourselves, we unconsciously believe that this person does not have what he or she needs and will unwittingly transmit this to him or her. In this case, neither the healer nor the person receiving healing is certain of Divine support and resistance takes over.

A former student once came to me for advice. He was having difficulty with a client. He said the person was going through very hard times, but he was unwilling to acknowledge how upset he was about what was going on. The student wanted to know how I would handle a case like this. I responded by helping him become aware that he was upset that his client was not going deep enough into his emotions.

This was upsetting him because he was telling himself that this meant he was not going to be able to help him, and his client was headed for a disaster. As long as my student unconsciously believed he would not be able to help this person, there was no amount of technique instruction I could give that would result in a different outcome. He was lost in a story about why his client would not own his emotions that included explanations like, "He is too much in his head...I don't work that well with these types of people...I guess it is not painful enough for him yet..." When I got him to disengage from the story and acknowledge the unconscious issue that told him that he could not help this person in remembrance, he had a breakthrough. Rather than subtly giving up and bracing for his client's painful future, he saw that it was time for him to take this person by the hand and show him exactly what was not working in a loving, but firm, way. With this inspiration, he was able to reach his client in a way that had eluded him previously. He also realized that he didn't need my advice. What he needed was someone to support him in acknowledging his issues in remembrance of the Divine.

Helping Others

No one can take on another's process for them. We must listen to what is troubling an individual without trying to change what is upsetting him or her. We are not trying to figure out why people are upset or what they need to do in order to not be upset. Rather, we support them in facing their problems and acknowledging their issues in remembrance.

The more comfortable we are with our own emotions, the

easier it is for us to hold other people when they are angry, sad, or frightened. When listening to what is upsetting others, it is important to make space in our heart for whatever they have to share. We are neither condoning nor condemning what they tell us. We are simply recognizing their feelings. Each of us is human. In order to help others, we must have room in our hearts for them to share difficult feelings and issues without judgment. Judgment is a tool of separation that we use to keep ourselves from whatever is uncomfortable for us. At the heart of every unpleasant feeling is a person who believes something about life that hurts. If people are not given the space to own their feelings and room to admit what is troubling them, these beliefs will not be uncovered and healed.

> *Gandhi once spoke about the inner battle all of us fight with our lower self. When asked about how he fared in that conflict, he replied, "Not very well." He then said that his own difficulty in this struggle is what helps him have compassion for all the other rascals out there.*

Many times, when people are helping another person, they take it on themselves to try to figure out how to make the person feel better. Or, they spend their time working on why people think they are in this situation (story) instead of helping them face what they are upset about. Usually, when people present for a healing, they ask us to help them discover or resolve why they are in these situations. They seldom ask us to help them through what is going on. The moment people begin to talk about why they are in certain situations or what they are doing that is causing their problems; they are in their story. It is the healer's job to help them face what is upsetting without becoming caught up in the stories. If people are upset, there is somewhere inside of them that they are not aware of divine support. They have decided that a given situation equals their suffering. This is what we are helping them to uncover

Once we have helped people identify and face what is upsetting them, we next help them become conscious of their experiences and what they believe this situation means. It is important that they feel their experience and become aware of the pain associated with their issues. We practice compassionate listening by recognizing their issues without giving advice or putting words in their mouth and encourage them to open in remembrance. We know that they have found their issue because it breaks their heart to say it and saddens our heart to hear it. If what they are saying about the situation were true, then the world would not be a very fulfilling place to be.

The people we are caring for may want to engage us in talking about their problems or issues, but we are only the fingers pointing at the moon, not the moon itself. The longer they are engaged with us talking about their issues, the less time they are reflecting in remembrance, where the real resolution is to be found. We continue pointing them in the direction of remembrance until they are at peace and we are convinced that they are resolved. If they are not completely at peace with what they receive from the Divine, we encourage them to face what is bothering them about it and find their next issue. They may sometimes think that they are finished, but we might notice that something they are sharing with us does not feel complete. This may be a blind spot for them. In this case, we lovingly inquire about what we are sensing, without pasting on our perceptions. If our sense of what is incomplete resonates with them, we can encourage them to continue the healing process. When they reach completion, time is spent in gratitude giving thanks for what was received in remembrance.

Learn from Every Healing

Spiritual healing is a way of moving through our issues and growing, but it is not the substance of what that transformation will look like. The beauty is in seeing what emerges when we support someone to come back into harmony with the Divine. It is just as important for the healer to surrender to the healing process as it is for the one who is receiving healing. There is no control in helping others. If we think we know how they should be or what their answers are, our ideas may be in the way of people getting what they need. It is not for them to become like us or respond in the way we would respond. It is to realize their own new creation.

Facilitating healing for others is a process of continuing education. We must be willing to approach healing with a student's mind and be open to learning new things. Each person is unique. While the steps we go through are similar, what these steps look like can vary greatly. Assisting others is an art that is learned by applying the steps of spiritual healing over time. We start with love and an intention to bring everything a person shares with us into communion with the Divine. After that, the rest is refinement.

Chapter Summary

1. Before starting any healing work, pray. Remind yourself of the ever-present support of the Divine, and align yourself with it. Ask that your heart, hands, eyes, ears, and speech be in service to the Divine and the other person's highest good.

2. Listen, become earth for the people you are assisting, and receive whatever they have to share. Listen for what is troubling them. Stay in remembrance, making space in your heart for whatever they have to say without judgment.

3. Encourage them to face what is upsetting them without trying to fix it, figure out why it is happening, or why they are upset.

4. Ask them what their problem means for them. What is their experience of what is happening? What do they believe it means for them?

5. Have them honestly assess how believing what their self tells them about the situation makes them feel. Encourage them to acknowledge their experience, and open in remembrance for support and guidance.

6. If they are at all unresolved after receiving support and guidance in remembrance, help them face what is troubling them and return to the fourth step.

7. After they reach a state of peace, both the healer and the healed can take some time in gratitude to the Divine for what they have received.

Exercise

Practice applying these seven steps with someone in your life. Let them know that you are practicing, and discuss the process with them before you begin. After you are finished, ask yourself what you learned about the process of healing in this exchange.

Chapter Ten

Living a Life of Connection

Stay with those people who do the hardest work of rarely
laying down the pick and shovel, that keep revealing our
deeper kinship with God.
—Hafiz

The last thing I would want anyone to leave this book with
is the idea that, if you are sick or struggling, it is because you are
doing something wrong. The whole point of this book is that
difficult things are a part of life and our connection to the
Divine is capable of carrying us through any of them. The
painful events of our lives help us grow in our experience of
God's love. The important question is not whether you struggle.
It is whether those struggles deepen your experience of the
Divine and free your spirit.

If all of our actions and experience are built on either an
awareness of connection or separation, then creating our lives to
be ones of connection is paramount to our fulfillment. I believe
the rituals and practices at the foundation of most religions are
designed to foster this connection. Right now, a trend of people
are trying to apply the principles of spirituality to their lives in
order to get more of what they want. I often refer to this as spiritual materialism. Rather than discovering sufficiency in what

we have been given and trusting the movement of the Divine, spirituality is treated like a tool. It would better to apply our lives to the principles of spirituality. This means we first connect our selves to spirit, come into harmony with the Divine, and then build our lives around that connection. The best way to do this is to adopt a spiritual path and set of practices.

It is said that there are as many paths to God as there are ways up a mountain. The important thing is that you take one and walk it. Follow the one you are attracted to and the one you see leading people to the top. You cannot follow yourself somewhere that you have never been. The road to God is the most subtle and exalted of all roads. Put yourself between the hands of a guide who can show you the way, not someone who says, "Be like me." Instead, choose someone who says, "I am nothing but a guide and servant to the divine reality." One who allows you to walk on his heart is the earth in which the flower of your spirit can grow.

I certainly did not set out to become a Sufi. I set out to find happiness. On the way, I found spirituality and Sufism to be the path that worked for me and continues to work to this day. All paths are simply a container for the teachings. They are not the water that quenches our spiritual thirst. The water is our direct, personal connection to the Divine that nurtures and uncovers our spirits. Make sure the container you are holding is filled with that water and is not an empty shell being carried and passed around by the thirsty. A famous remark of the people of inside, to those who carry only the outside religion, is, "You take your religion dead from the dead, while we take ours alive from the Living One.

The job of a spiritual path or religion is to teach us how to orient our lives to finding and drinking the living water of spirit. While the requirements of a spiritual path are only the container that holds the living water, without that container, the water would drain away. We must learn to discover the difference between the requirements of a path triggering our issues and something truly not working for us. Many of the practices and requirements of a spiritual path or religion may rub up against what we prefer for ourselves. It is important to remember, however, that what we are attracted to in these paths is not yet consciously contained in our selves, so a certain amount of friction is inevitable. What we do in these moments of friction will determine how far along the path we travel.

Nurturing Our Spirit

Developing our spirits requires both purification and growth. Like a seed, we must first purify it from everything that is alien to it and place it in an environment in which it will flourish. The height of wisdom is in knowing the difference between what is good for us from what is bad for us. That information is to be found with the Divine. In order to refine our spiritual nature, we must live in a pure way. If we are busy following our desire nature, the still, small voice inside is drowned out by the energy and activities that lead us away from reflection. The poet Hafiz reminds us:

> We cannot discern the subtle science of Divinity until we
> silence the barking dog between our own legs.

For some of us, the barking dog is in our wallets. For others, it is in our stomachs. For some, it is in position and esteem. The outer practices and requirements of a spiritual path are meant to enable us to establish a middle way between excess and self-denial. All of us need support, provision, affection, food, and acknowledgement, but a spiritual path helps us be in right relationship with these things. A path tells us what will feed or harm our spiritual awareness. Following this guidance creates an environment in which we can grow. It is like a brace on a young tree. The brace is there to help the tree grow strong and straight. It also keeps it from being knocked over by the winds of life. When the tree is strong enough to stand on its own, the brace is no longer needed because the tree can now stand straight under its own power.

I believe the spiritual paths that were given to people through the various prophets and messengers throughout history were sent to explain to us what was good for our natures and would lead to the flowering of our spirit. It is no good to pour water on a seed if it is not held in the ground of what is wholesome for it. True spirituality must contain both an inner connection to the living water and an outer adherence to moral principles. Ultimately, we experience this inner and outer dimension as two sides of the same coin. The inner side is the state of being that results from a living connection to God. The outer side is how a person in that state of being interacts with the things in his or her life. Having a living connection with God gives us the necessary insight and wisdom to be in the right relationship with the things of our lives. We see them for what they are and know the difference between what leads to our beautification and what brings us low.

A spiritual path can provide the direction, but we have to provide the locomotion. A jewel becomes evident through much polishing. Over time, the application of spiritual practices and principles leads to arrival. When I first met my teacher, I was so impressed and attracted to the amount of peace he carried in his heart. Everything from the way he cared for those who were suffering to the way he made himself available to everyone who needed him touched my heart. The balance and grace contained within his state of being brought tears to my eyes. One of the senior teachers in the Sufi order that I follow reminded me that what I was beholding was the product of a system that had been assiduously applied. He pointed out what I was seeing was the result of years of living for and drinking the living water of spirit.

The spiritual path we choose to walk becomes the ship that carries us from the shore of separation to the shore of unity and experiencing the Divine in all things. It is the ship, not the shore. It is important not to lose sight of this and allow our path to become our Lord. Only when we reach that shore will we truly become the expression of outer and inner balance. This is when we become the living embodiment of our path. We then find ourselves acting in accordance with our spiritual path and not because it says so. Rather, it is because that is how a person in a state of connection behaves. This embodiment is living on the shore of connection and the fruit of the path. We do not plant apple trees for the sake of having a tree. It is for the apples that result from all of our labors. If we follow teachers that embody only planting and laboring, our spirits will continue to go hungry. It is the embodied knowledge that comes from a realized teacher that attracts our hearts and spirits. The greatest advice I can give is to find a path and a teacher that carries these qualities and follow their guidance.

Some of the people I have worked with have decided to

walk the Sufi path. Others have shared that working through this process has helped them to better understand their own religions. The way we choose to walk is a personal decision. My teacher continually reminds us that, if all religions knew their religion well, there would be only one religion, that is, the religion of love, peace, mercy, justice, and freedom.

Chapter Summary

1. The foundation of everything we do is either built on an experience of connection or separation from the Divine.
2. Understanding this, we must construct our lives around our spiritual connection, not the other way around.
3. The best way to do this is to find a spiritual path that we are attracted to and feel supports us.
4. A spiritual path should orient us to the living water of divine connection, not just to outer practice and ceremony.
5. It is important not to stop walking our path just because the requirements rub up against our desire nature.
6. The point of any path is to lead you to a destination with the Divine.
7. When you reach that destination, you become the path that you walk and discover an inner and outer balance.

Exercise

Do you have a spiritual practice in place to connect to the Divine every day? If not, create one. Think about this practice. Is it the foundation of your life? Is it something you fit into your day? If it is something you try to fit in, practice making it your first priority and see how your life changes.

Chapter Eleven

Walking Forward

If you want glory that does not fade,
then do not glory in a glory that fades
—Ibn Ata'illah

The lessons of this book are simple ones. Face what is troubling us, acknowledge our issues, remind our selves of Divine support, and take the time to receive from this source until we are at peace. Simple, however, doesn't always mean easy. In the beginning, many of these practices seem counterintuitive. Instead of running from what hurts, we face and feel it. Instead of trying to manage our painful experiences, we acknowledge them and realize they are the call that attracts Divine response. Instead of focusing on the outside and what we feel is expected of us, we turn inside and care first and foremost for our experience.

This process could be summed up as living a life without resistance. In each moment, we are given what we need, but it is only by repeatedly going through this process that we realize how little we understand what our real needs are. Spiritual healing is not a process of becoming great. It is a process of realizing the greatness of the Divine and flourishing under that care. Each step becomes a new discovery. Wonder and awe replace our ideas of where we think we are headed or what our lives should look like.

The most challenging and rewarding journey we can take is one of beautifying our own selves. The objections of our lower nature however are many. The explanations of our resistance are convincing. The reasons not to surrender are well-documented, and most of the world is not all that supportive. They don't offer classes on it in high school, and many of us don't have all that much experience going inside. All of this would be reason enough not to take the trip if it weren't for that restless spirit inside of us that demands more.

Our conscious journey home begins with the intention to live a fulfilling, harmonious, and beautiful life. It is an intention that we repeatedly return to. This intention brings to light anything in our lives that doesn't measure up to our heart's desires. We begin to take issue with the parts of our lives that are unsatisfying and reach out for more. We realize our selves do not know how to reach the fulfillment we seek and we take our Creator as our guide.

Although the journey is not an easy one, we don't have to make it alone. More and more people are waking up and answering the call of their spirits. Businesses and organizations are beginning to redefine what bottom-line success really means. People in health care are realizing that healing is more than just not hurting. Individuals everywhere are seeking harmony in their lives and relationships. It is an accepted practice among my community, that if we cannot resolve an issue on our own in 48 hours, then we reach out to a friend for help. The importance of individuals, supporting each other on their journeys cannot be overstated.

As a healer, business consultant, and workshop leader, I have had the blessing of being a part of this return to spirit.

The programs and classes we offer are designed to bring together like-minded people and provide them the resources to not only achieve personal healing but to become a source of support to others in this world. If the ideas contained in this book have touched your heart, inspired you, or confirmed what you already knew, then a prayer of mine has been answered.

If you would like to continue the journey of spiritual healing, many resources are available to you. You can start by visiting my Web site at www.howtowalkwithGod.com. There, you can sign up for a monthly newsletter that contains further teachings and stories of people just like you who are walking in this way. You can order instructional CDs and find a spiritual healer or workshop in your area by visiting our resource center and calendar of events. For those of you who are interested in business and organizational healing, you can find resources and classes through LionHeart Consulting. We are on the Web at www.lionheart.com

The teachings I have shared here are ones I am continually learning on deeper and deeper levels. It seems that all of my greatest realizations come back to simple truths, and I am once again reminded of the difference between knowing a thing in my mind and experiencing it in my heart. This book, however, was not written to teach you things. Rather, it was to point you to a way of living. What you will experience as you walk with God, how those experiences will move you, and what expression that relationship will take is unique to you. As I come to a close, I am humbly reminded of what the Sufi poet, Rumi, said,

Nothing I say can explain to you Divine Love
Yet all of creation cannot seem to stop talking about it

May this book be a light to you on your journey home.

Quick Order Form

To order more copies of this book or to find out about other products visit www.howtowalkwithGod.com.

To order by mail please send this form to:
Rosewood press
99 Rosewood Ln.
Berkeley Springs, WV 25411

I would like to order_____ copies of Walking with God at 15.95 each

Name _____
Address_____
City _____State_____
Zip_____
Telephone_____
Email _____

Shipping by Air
U.S. add $4.00
International add $9.00
Payment
Check ____ Credit Card _____
Card Name_____
Card Number _____ Expiration _____
Name as it appears on Card _____